Cultural Awareness
for Young Children

Cultural Awareness for Young Children

Revised Edition

Earldene McNeill, Instructor of Child Development, Eastfield College, Mesquite, Texas

Judy Allen, Teacher and Administrator at the Learning Tree, Dallas, Texas

Velma Schmidt, Ed.D., Professor of Education, Early Childhood Education, North Texas State University, Denton, Texas

Barbara McNeill Brierton, Illustrations and Artistic Translations

The Learning Tree
Dallas, Texas

The Learning Tree
9998 Ferguson Road
Dallas, Texas 75228

Library of Congress Catalog No. 75-34504

ISBN 0-940908-00-X

Design: Cynthia Fowler
Typesetting: Ellis Graphics
Printing: Edwards Brothers

PREFACE

More than ten years ago some families in Dallas came together to share their ideas on awareness and understanding of the cultures in Texas and in the United States. The idea for a school for young children developed out of this discussion—one that would integrate cultural awareness into the program. Hence, the Learning Tree was established. The teachers searched for authentic information about cultures from books and films, and they talked to people from each culture in their community. The creative activities and information in this book reflect the program for cultural awareness. As the children experience each culture each year, the teachers revise their program. The approach in this book demonstrates one way young children can become culturally aware.

A major concern of the authors is the lack of acceptance of the diversity of the traditional customs and lifestyles of a culture by many of the citizens of this country. For many years, a major goal in the United States was the "melting pot" philosophy. The idea was to "melt" all cultures into a new American lifestyle. What we failed to realize, was the strength of each heritage. The melting pot idea did not work. If we can help children and families develop an appreciation for all cultures, be they the same or different, so that each individual can retain the customs of his ethnic identity, then some progress toward harmony will have been made.

To accomplish an acceptance of diversity, adults working with young children need to be aware of their stereotypic views of cultures and share authentic information about each culture with children. Racist attitudes need to be changed to positive feelings toward others. Discussions about "we and they" need to be changed to "us." The non-minority person must inform her children about the contributions and strengths of cultures in our society. As your culture and ours are valued by others, our own feelings about our ethnic heritage become that of pride; and our self-image is enhanced.

We recommend that you use this book in the context of a cultural experience. Combine the information in the book with the activities so that the children begin to understand something about the total life of the culture. Help children see ethnic groups as part of the modern world. Help them separate how cultures lived in the past from the way they live today. Add additional authentic information. Make it your responsibility to give children accurate information about ethnic groups. Invite members of each culture to your classroom.

Evaluate pictures and books and other materials about cultures before you use them. Most of the publications written about ten years ago or more, were not accurate. Many of these publications gave a stereotyped view of the culture. In recent years, more of the new publications give more authentic information and a more positive image of the cultures. One reason for this change is that authors from each culture are writing the books.

Keep abreast about the current happenings in the cultures in your community and in our country. Inform yourself of the variations within each culture and of the differences in customs in various sections of the United States. Be aware of the continuing changes in customs and traditions.

The major goal of the authors is that information and activities in this book serve as an influence in accepting diversity and pluralism. If people can live together like a tossed salad, keeping their individual cultural identity while at the same time working and living together in harmony, some progress will have been made. As harmony and understanding of each other increase, our country and all its citizens will be enriched.

CONTENTS

INTRODUCTION

Informal Education

The philosophy of the Learning Tree is that learning is effective when each child works on his level of success in an atmosphere which encourages learning without pressure. Pressure leads to frustration. Many levels of learning are happening at the same time. The plans of teachers are flexible enough to use the interests and questions of children for activities. The atmosphere is informal—activity is going on in all or most of the learning centers at the same time.

An informal atmosphere is based on the belief that children can learn to work actively with a minimum of limits or rules. Some limits and routines are necessary. Within these limits, children move about freely in their active learning to accomplish their own goals. They can learn to do this without interfering with the activities of others. They may choose to work alone or in small groups.

The important factors in informal learning at the Learning Tree are individualization, independent learning and the arrangement of the environment into learning centers. To be effective, a program must include these three factors and be supported by an understanding of the developmental growth of young children by adults and parents.

Child Development

An informal program requires that learning experiences be based on the developmental characteristics of children. The program at the Learning Tree is based on the characteristics of children ages three through six.

The basic principle of child development is that each child is a unique human being. Each child has her own developmental timetable. She grows and learns at her own rate. Each child comes to school at her own level of functioning. Each child has her own interests. The program must be flexible enough to help each child be a successful learner—allowing for a wide range of learning levels and rates of development.

Young children of this age are very active—their muscles develop through activity and they want to see, feel, touch, taste and listen to everything in their environment. Children learn through their activity and their senses. They may rest when they are tired, and work when their energy is renewed through relaxation and nutritious snacks.

Since the young child is very active and he acts before he thinks, he often socializes physically. If he wants another child to play with him, he pulls him by the arm or makes his request in some physical way. With adult suggestions, he begins to learn that he is much more successful with language—that he can enjoy being with other children and engage in activities using language. Thus, when experiences with other children are pleasant, many social interactions occur each day.

Social interactions necessitate language. Language is also an important key to learning throughout life. For the young child, development of oral language is essential. No child should be expected to learn to read words which are not in his speaking vocabulary. Therefore, the Learning Tree provides the freedom for children to extend their language by talking to each other, by hearing and creating stories and poems and by the variety of experiences provided throughout the year, especially the "cultural awareness" experiences. Each new experience adds new words to the child's speaking vocabulary. The environment of the Learning Tree has many objects and materials which children can handle and manipulate and talk about. Learning activities from which children may select give the children opportunity to experience the "real thing" or to role play.

Young children are not able to do abstract thinking, thinking without the experience, so it is essential that a program for this age be based on real experiences and concrete materials. Whether the child is engaged in art, numbers, science or the letters of the alphabet, he first manipulates and experiments with materials in his environment. After he has had many "hands-on" experiences, he will gradually connect this understanding to the symbols—letters and words. For many children, success and understanding of the symbolic level occurs after the age of six or seven.

The first school experience for young children provides opportunities to live and to work with other children of similar ages. Grouping children of several ages together, multi-age grouping, sets the stage for learning from each other and for helping each other.

The younger the child, the more ego-centric or self-centered she is; that is, she thinks how what she does or what is done to her will affect only herself. As she lives with other children and adults in the give-and-take world of school, she is able to consider how her actions will affect the other children. Gradually, her thinking matures so that she can understand how the other children feel.

Independent Learning

As the child begins school, he is very dependent on the adults. As he learns the routines and the basic skills, such as cutting and using art materials, he becomes more independent. Learning by young children is a continual process of receiving help from adults as needed so that they develop into children who learn much by working independently.

Independence also means being able to solve their own problems, knowing that adult help is always available. Problems involve settling disagreements with others, deciding which materials to use for a project and sharing equipment with other children. To solve a problem, different solutions are considered and a choice is made. The results often prove to be unsatisfactory, and another solution must be tried. The more problem-solving experiences children have, the better judgments they learn to make. The creative activities and the opportunity to make choices at the Learning Tree give the children practice in learning to solve problems and to make decisions.

Individualization

The concept of "individual differences" is basic to an individualized program. Each child begins at her own developmental level, learns at her own rate and remains with one activity for as long as she is able to benefit from it. No two children are alike in their level, their rate and the amount of time they spend on one activity.

An individualized approach means that each child is working at her level of success. A child who is working at her level is successful and is generally motivated to try new activities. Success indicates to a child indirectly that learning is a satisfying activity and that he has the ability to learn. The one-to-one relationship between the child and the adult provides the emotional support and security each child needs at this age. The adult responds to the level of each child, to her style of learning and to her interests.

Individualization is not confined to a one-to-one teaching/learning situation. Small groups with a similar interest meet. They may gather because they want to listen to a specific story or to share something brought from home. At times the activity is interesting to all children. Large group activities planned with children include plans for the day, stories, games, music, dances and special concerns of the school family. Problems are solved together. Children and adults meet when they need each other—when there is a common interest, a celebration or a visitor.

The professional adult has many roles in the informal classroom. This adult may be a director or teacher working with aides, parents or volunteers. The adult is an observer, a listener, a facilitator and a director.

As an observer, the adult learns to know the personality, strengths and interests of each child. On the basis of this information, equipment and materials are placed in the environment to extend the interests of individual children. Records are made of the progress and activities of each child. The observer sees how children solve their own problems and how they help each other. As a listener, the adult listens patiently to the interaction of children, the ideas and concepts the children are trying to understand, their levels of language development, the concerns that affect the emotions of the children, and asks questions which lead to ways of finding the answers. As a facilitator, the alert adult decides when to help children solve their problems and when to let them solve problems themselves, when to encourage a child into an activity and when to let him think or rest, when to ask a child a question to extend his thinking and when not to interrupt his concentration, and when to add materials to the environment to encourage learning and when to remove them. As a director, the adult plans the environment so that learning can take place, keeps parents informed of the development and growth of their child, plans field trips, invites resource persons, encourages the growth and education of parents and others who help in the classroom, plans daily activities that may interest some of the children and introduces new ideas with concrete materials.

The adults support each child through periods of sensitivity in which he awakens as an individual with a curiosity that motivates him to explore and to investigate. Learning centers permit such investigation to take place.

Learning Centers

The indoor-outdoor environment is arranged into learning centers. The equipment and materials that relate to one area of interest are organized in one learning center. The adults help children learn how to use the equipment, how to take care of it and how to put it away. The learning centers help children develop:

- Social skills in the give-and-take of getting along with one another
- Coordination of large and small muscles
- Creativity and imagination in the use of a variety of materials in their own way

- Emotional stability through guidance and the experience of living in a group
- Language as they talk, plan, share and ask questions
- The idea of reading through symbolizing their own language
- An understanding of the world around them as they dramatize the adult roles and as they reconstruct the world with raw materials
- The ability to solve their problems of living and learning
- Concepts of color, size, shape and space

The learning centers are:

- Family Living
- Nature/Science
- Blocks
- Music/Dance
- Art
- Books/Pictures
- Woodworking
- Manipulatives and Games
- Outdoor

Creativity

One important goal at the Learning Tree is to keep creativity alive and spontaneous. Young children will create often if they have the freedom to do so. Elements in creativity are a variety of materials, time and acceptance of their ideas. Many different kinds of materials are available in the room. Children are not told what to make or which materials to use. They may or may not make an item that has been introduced or discussed; and if they decide to create something, they select from the available materials. Some children find materials outdoors or they may find other things at home and bring them to school the next day. Large blocks of time allow opportunity to work out an idea. Whether the final product is complicated or simple, it is accepted by the adults. The final product is not as important as the process the child uses in thinking, planning, trying out different ways and finally creating something to his own satisfaction.

Children create in many ways. They make their own rules for games. They dictate or print their own stories, plays and poems; and make their own books. They create their own dances and new verses to songs. They create masks, other crafts and pictures. They build with tools or with blocks. Damp sand and mud provide the materials for many new creations. The photographs and ideas in this book illustrate the many ways the children create at the Learning Tree. The stress on creativity is especially desirable when children participate in cultural awareness.

Parent Participation

An important part of a program for young children is open communication and close relationships with parents. Parents must be a part of the experiences of their child in school. Participation of parents in the classroom and on field trips; and in sharing their talents, hobbies and interests, help build a close relationship. An active but informal parent group is a tremendous asset to a program. Monthly meetings, where parents feel comfortable and free to express themselves, and where they are kept informed of the activities of the school, are social as well as educational activities. Informal gatherings meet the needs of parents and give them opportunities to discuss problems and topics of interest to them and to share ideas with other parents and adults. Periodic parent-teacher conferences on the development of the child help parents understand the growth of their child. Parents and teachers can work as partners through participation, meetings and conferences.

Resource persons are invited to come to school to show children how they make jewelry and pottery, and how they carve items out of wood. Parents, with the help of the children, cook foods that are representative of their culture. A favorite activity is eating the food parents have prepared.

Mothers and fathers help in the classroom one day a month. Parents accompany children on field trips. A study group of mothers from the Learning Tree began as an informal social coffee hour. They decided to meet regularly to study topics of their choice and to help the school. A food cooperative developed out of these meetings.

Some activities include the entire family. For example, parents and children enjoy Mexican and soul food dinners as a part of the experiences of these cultures. The End of the Trail cook-out, involving all of the families, is an annual event ending the school year. Dinners and other cultural experiences are ways to help parents and children develop an awareness of other American cultures.

Cultural Awareness

This book documents the portion of the program of the Learning Tree which attempts to develop an awareness of American cultures. Many other goals and themes included in the program have been omitted from this publication.

The school was designed to bring together families from many ethnic backgrounds. One goal of the Learning Tree is that children learn to appreciate and accept all people as a result of their daily experiences with these children and their families.

Some young children today have opportunities to associate with children of other cultures in their neighborhoods, schools, churches and communities. The cultural themes throughout the year are the "beginning" of a lifetime of awareness of the richness other cultures add to our society. The seeds of this awareness are shown in this program. The lifestyles, the foods and the customs of each culture are shared. The "hands-on" approach is used as indicated by the activities in this book. The school environment has artifacts, pictures and many other items to create an atmosphere representing a particular culture. Natives of each culture are invited to share an aspect of their culture. Children role play the customs and games they learn. The costumes and cultural items they make are worn in their dramatic activities, and this adds a reality to the role playing. The dramatizing of roles is one way to begin to understand a culture. Through the suggested activities in this book, in addition to meeting families of the different cultures, children will begin to appreciate the rich diversity of customs and contributions from the many cultures in America. The child will add to this understanding year by year. Hopefully, these experiences will be a beginning of a lifetime of appreciation of American cultures.

Children have the option of whether or not they will become involved in these cultural themes. Some children involve themselves completely while other participate in selected activities which capture their interests. Occasionally, a child will not be interested in any of the cultures and consequently chooses not to participate. Other materials and activities are always available for these children. Quiet places and activities are available for the child who wants to do something else. The flexibility in the program allows for individual interests and many different levels of skills.

A first cultural event for parents and children at the Learning Tree is a social evening with a dinner. The parents share their own cultural backgrounds. They discuss how the customs and lifestyles of their present family compare to that of their family when they were children. The discussions help parents understand the great influence the culture of their parents had on their values and the cultural changes they have made as parents. The parents share food they enjoyed as children and discuss how the present American culture affects their children. When children learn to love and to respect each other, the attitudes of the parents are also influenced. A related goal of cultural awareness is that through studying the contributions of American cultures, the children will develop an appreciation and understanding of their own culture.

The suggestions for learning about the American cultures include authentic information to the extent this can be determined—information that provides the child with a realistic picture of that culture. An attempt has been made to omit books and pictures that present a false and stereotyped view of a culture.

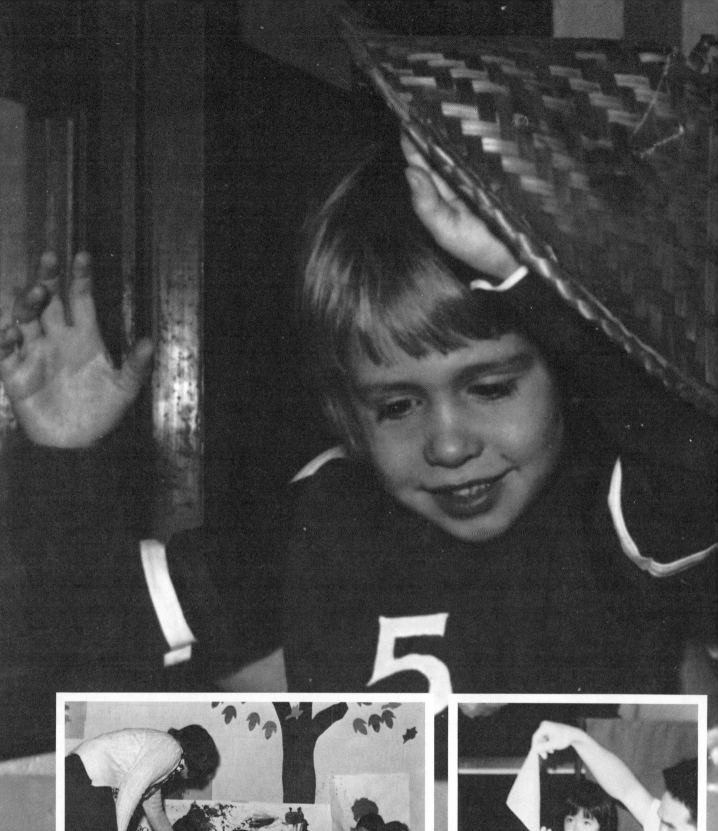

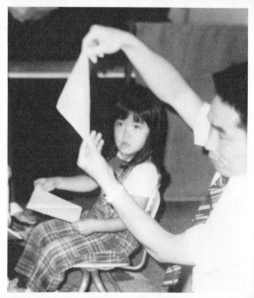

Asian Cultures

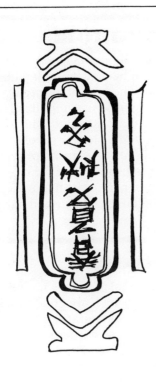

Asian American, Chinese and Japanese Heritage

The customs of the Asian cultures are very different from the ways American children live. They delight in imitating them. To pretend to be a Chinese woman on the way to the buraku, to build a junk for fishing or to dive for pearls in the Ise Bay, are dramatized by children at the Learning Tree.

Asian cultures, as described in this book, are mainly that of China and Japan. However, the concepts and ideas can be extended to all cultures of the Far East. Young children of Japanese and Chinese cultural backgrounds can identify with, and appreciate their own cultural heritage. Young children of other cultures become familiar with another way of living. Books about the Vietnamese are included in the bibliography at the end of this chapter.

FAMILY LIVING

Homes

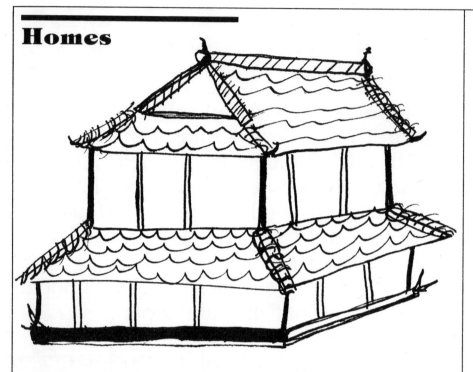

Some Asian homes have roofs made of tile and others have thatched roofs. The inside walls of the traditional Japanese homes are sliding doors made of paper. These walls are called shoji (SHOjee).

A room with paper walls can be constructed by attaching one end of a 36" wide roll of butcher paper to one wall. Stretch the paper across the room, around a card table or chair, and attach to another wall to make an enclosure. Children cut doors in the paper wall.

In the family center, include low tables, pillows and tatamis on the floor. Children and adults take off shoes before entering this area. In the center of the area, children can make a square fire pit by placing bricks in a one-foot square.

Tokonoma

The tokonoma is a special place of beauty in the Japanese home. The love of nature by the Japanese is symbolized with a flower arrangement and a display of a picture-scroll.

Children take turns providing objects from nature for this place of beauty. It helps them appreciate the beauty in nature.

Gardens

Most Asian homes include gardens which are created with plants, rocks, statues and pools. These gardens are considered works of art.

Children select a place out-of-doors to create a garden. They select rocks, small trees or bushes and add a container of water placed in a shallow hole prepared by children. Add wind bells to the garden scene. Child cuts six twelve-inch strings. Tie one end of each string to a bell. Tie the other end of the string to a coat hanger, one inch apart and hang in a gentle wind.

Clothing

Japanese and Chinese articles available for role playing:

coolie hats
capes
chopsticks
paper fans
kimonos
futon
tea cups
umbrellas

clogs
tatamis
tea pot
kabuki hand puppets
getas
koheshi dolls
lacquer ware

Ikebana

The Japanese have a unique art of arranging flowers. Have pictures and resource books available that will acquaint the child with Japanese flower arranging. Children pick fresh flowers, leaves and greenery. Also, provide artificial flowers, vases and clay. Using these materials, children arrange flowers and greenery to appear as if they are growing.

Bonsai

Bonsai or tray planting is an art that started in Japan. Children imitate the Bonsai method by planting small plants in shallow containers.

Buraku

A buraku is a group of small shops, including a general store, where villagers buy food, dishes and clothing.

Children set up a general store where Japanese and Chinese items, such as fans and lanterns, can be purchased with play money.

Inexpensive items, such as fold-out paper fans, toys, chopsticks and small paper umbrellas, can also be purchased at import shops for the general store. "Made in Japan" items are available at variety stores. Children take turns being the store owner and the shoppers. Flowers made by children may be added to the store. Cherry blossoms, iris, chrysanthemums and azaleas originally came from Japan and could be added to the general store. Also, add any items that have been created by children, such as clothing, kites, pottery and flags. Suggestions for creating items are on the following pages.

Foods

Rice

Hot rainy weather in southern China is the climate needed for growing tea and rice.

Asians eat rice at every meal. Cook rice, following the directions on the package. Children participate in the whole process—measuring, stirring and serving. While the rice is cooking, children recall what they did. Print the recipe on a chart. Some children copy the recipe and take it home. Rice is served in small bowls and eaten with chopsticks.

Raw Fish

Buy kipper-snacks at the grocery store. Eat them as a substitute for raw fish. Some children eat raw fish dipped in soy sauce.

Fortune Cookies

4 egg whites
1 cup sugar
½ cup melted butter
¼ cup flour

¼ teaspoon salt
½ teaspoon vanilla
2 tablespoons water

Write fortunes or messages on strips of paper. Fold them. Mix sugar into the egg whites and blend until fluffy. Melt the butter and cool it so it's not too hot. Add flour, salt, vanilla, water and butter to the sugar mixture. Beat until the batter is smooth. Grease a cookie sheet very well. Pour batter from a spoon to form circles (about 3" or 8 cm.). Bake at 375° for about 8 minutes. Lay a message on each circle, fold it in thirds, then bend it gently in the center. If the cookies get too hard to bend, put them back in the oven for a minute.

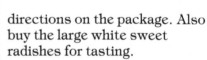

Fruits & Vegetables

Bring canned or frozen Chinese and Japanese vegetables and tangerines for a tasting experience. Prepare frozen vegetables according to directions on the package. Also buy the large white sweet radishes for tasting.

Tea

Children have a Japanese tea party—sitting on cushions around a low table. Buy jasmine or green tea and brew it in a small teapot. Children serve each other using small cups without handles. Serve with fortune cookies which are specially made for children. Or make fortune cookies, following this recipe.

CREATIVE ART EXPRESSION

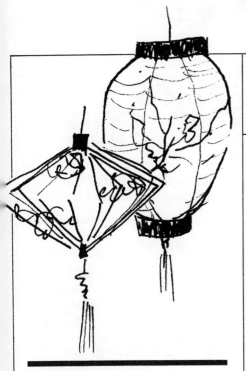

The ability of the Asian craftsmen and artists is shown in the hanging scrolls, portraits, porcelain and lacquer objects, silk robes, and calligraphy or brush writing.

Junks

Japanese fisherman use small boats called junks. Children make junks out of a variety of materials: wood scraps, cardboard, styrofoam. They then experiment to find out if their junks will float.

Lanterns

To make a lantern, fold a piece of 9" x 12" colored construction paper in half, lengthwise. Lay the paper so the fold is at the bottom. Draw a line one inch from the top across the paper. Cut slits, approximately one inch apart, from the fold to the line. Open and staple the 9" sides together. Make a handle for hanging from a 1" x 5" strip of paper. Attach the handle to one end of the lantern. Some children draw pictures on the paper before cutting the slits.

Flags

The design of the Japanese flag is a crimson (deep red) ball on a white background.

To make the flag, cut an 8½" x 11" sheet of white fabric or paper. Paint or color a crimson ball in the center of the flag and attach it to a 20" stick.

By LeeAnn

Coolie Hats

Coolie hats are wide-brimmed hats worn by Japanese farmers as protection from the rain. In China, the hats of the rice and wheat farmers are similar to an American beach hat.

To make a coolie hat, cut a circle about 18" in diameter. Cut one slit from the edge to the center. Overlap ends to form a cone-shaped coolie hat. Staple ends together.

Fans

Beautiful hand-painted fans are popular in China and Japan.

Take one 9" x 12" piece of construction paper. Lay the

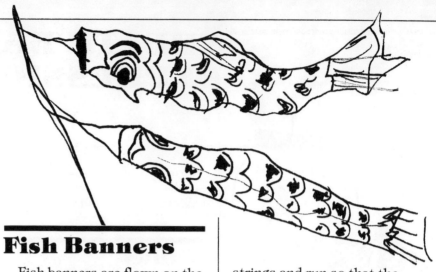

paper so that the 11" length is at the bottom. Children draw a picture on the paper, as is the custom in Asian countries. Fold the paper in accordion-pleated style, with the 9" width at the bottom. Staple the pleats together at one end, or tie them with a ribbon so that the child can hold the fan.

Capes

A cape is a piece of clothing worn by farmers as protection from rain when working in the rice fields. Make a cape from a piece of 36" x 36" cloth. Attach a tie to two of the corners of the cloth. Tie around the neck.

Fish Banners

Fish banners are flown on the boys' festival. (See Special Events in this chapter for a description of this holiday.) Use white lunch sacks to make fish banners. Children draw features of a fish on the sides of the sacks. Tie a string to each side of the sack. Hold the strings and run so that the "fish" sack catches the wind.

Kites

The dragon is the traditional emblem of China. A small group of children can make a large dragon kite. Each child draws and cuts a part of the dragon's body on paper. Attach these pieces to each other with pipe cleaners. To create interest for this activity, read the following books:

- LEE LON FLIES A KITE
- THE EMPEROR'S KITE
- LET'S TRAVEL IN CHINA

Pottery

Asian pottery and porcelain are beautiful works of art.

Young children make dishes of clay. They paint some of them with red, green, blue and gold colored tempera paint.

Bag

Silk scarves are used for carrying objects. The four corners of a square piece of fabric are tied together to carry belongings.

Getas

Japanese wear getas, a slipper made of wood, straw or rubber. Wooden getas are worn out-of-doors.

To make getas, children put their feet on a piece of cardboard and draw around them. Cut out the feet. Staple a strip of fabric to each side of the shoe and to the point between the big toe and the second toe. The strips hold the getas on the child's feet.

Obis

At one time, all Japanese women wore obis, a wide sash, with their kimonos as part of their dress. Today, kimonos with obis are worn for special occasions by most of the women in Japan.

Children tie a wide strip of bright-colored cloth, a yard long, around their waist over a kimono.

Origami

Some children are successful in the activity of origami, the Japanese art of folding paper. They fold flowers and animal figures. Buy packets of Japanese origami paper at import shops. Colored paper, thin enough for folding easily, may also be used. Several books on origami are listed in the bibliography at the end of this chapter.

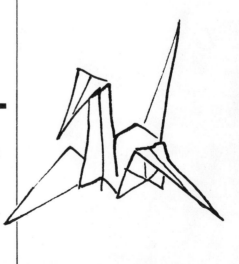

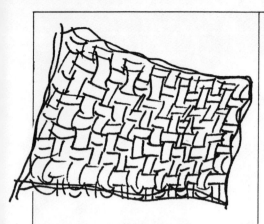

Tatamis

A tatami, a straw mat, is a floor-covering in Japanese homes. Getas and shoes are always taken off at the door to prevent soiling the tatami. Japanese people wear special slippers inside their homes.

Make tatamis by weaving strips of paper. Cut one piece of construction paper 12" x 18". Cut slits similar to those in making the lantern. For strips for weaving, cut strips 1" x 18" of paper. Weave the strips through the slits in the large piece of paper. Staple the ends of the strips to hold them in place.

Painting Banners

Chinese paintings show delicate impressions of dragons, ladies, bamboo and blossoms.

Imitating the Chinese finger painters, children use watercolors to draw with their fingers. They can paint on a 12" x 36" scroll. A scroll is a long piece of paper that has designs and writing on it. It is rolled up for storing. Some scrolls, kakemonos, have only writing on them. The writing is a message added to the drawing or painting.

Symbols:
- The PEACH TREE is a symbol of long life
- PLUM BLOSSOMS are a symbol of winter
- The CHRYSANTHEMUM is a symbol of autumn

Children also paint Chinese characters or letters on large sheets of white paper with black paint. This painting is known as calligraphy.

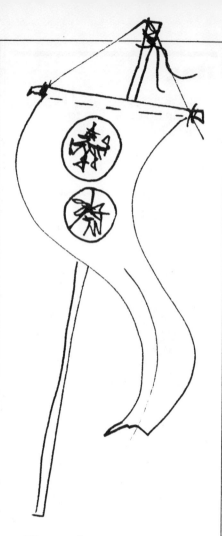

Watercolor pictures are painted with different sizes of brushes.

NATURE AND SCIENCE

Exploring the natural resources of Asian cultures may mean discovering the art of creating pearls, growing bean sprouts, raising silk worms and learning to make a cage for a cricket. These activities capture the interest of young children, promote hobbies and also suggest experiences outside the classroom.

Silkworms

Plan to introduce the Asian cultures and raising of silkworms when mulberry leaves are available. Parents as well as children delight in this adventure.

Place the eggs in a large glass container, aquarium or fish bowl. After the eggs hatch into worms, place a piece of nylon net over the opening of the container. Silkworms must be fed mulberry leaves every day. They eat on the mulberry leaves continuously until time for spinning the cocoon, about three weeks. The silkworm secretes a fluid which hardens into silk thread. The worm winds this thread around itself to form a cocoon. When the moths come out of the cocoon, in about three weeks, the children are eager to observe the process of reproduction and the laying of new eggs. To store the eggs for next year, place the eggs in an air-tight container in refrigerator. Read about silkworms in a children's encyclopedia.

Beautiful dresses, shirts and blouses are made of cloth woven from silk thread. Show clothing to the children.

Paper Making

To make recycled paper, use two frames with a piece of screen stapled to each frame. Tear old newspaper and soak it in warm water. Mix it with the water so that you have a pulp. Place frames on top of each other with the screen side up. Put the frames into the wet water to get the paper pulp on the frame. Take the frame out of the water, smooth the paper pulp, and drain. Put the frame, upside down, on paper towels. The pulp will be on the paper towel. Use a sponge to dry the screen side. Take the screen off the paper towel and use more paper towels to dry the pulp. Remove the paper towels from the recycled paper. Iron the square of paper with a medium warm iron. Children paint or mark on the paper. This Chinese method of paper making as we know it today is adapted by Ann Wiseman. See bibliography.

Bean Sprouts

A common Asian food is bean sprouts.

To grow bean sprouts, plant dried beans in small containers. Transplant some of the seedlings to the outdoor garden. Cut and taste the other bean sprouts.

Put dried lentils into a large container. Cover the beans with a wet paper towel. Keep the paper towel moist. The lentils sprout very soon. Children eat

Bamboo

Bamboo is a strong plant used to make chopsticks, baskets and umbrellas; and it is also used for food.

Show bamboo to the children and talk about how it grows and how it is used. Open a can of bamboo shoots and have a tasting party. Talk about how they taste. Look for other things made of bamboo.

the sprouts during the week as they sprout.

Bring a can of bean sprouts for tasting.

Crickets

Children in Japan hunt for crickets. They put the crickets into small cages and listen to their song.

Display a small cricket cage and go hunting for crickets. Put them into the cage.

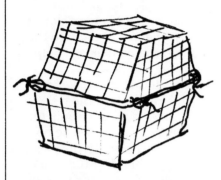

Some children make their own cages for crickets from small berry baskets and pipe cleaners. Place tops of two baskets together. Fasten rims of the baskets together with the pipe cleaners.

Cultured Pearls

A pearl forms inside an oyster shell when other things get inside the shell. The Japanese who work at the pearl farms in Ise Bay prepare the oysters in a special way so that they produce pearls.

Children make goggles to wear as they dramatize the adventure of the one who dives into the water for pearls.

Make goggles from the plastic holder from a six-pack of twelve-ounce canned drinks. One holder makes three sets of goggles. Cut the holder into three sections, two attached circles in each section. Tie strings to each side and tie around head.

Fish

Japan leads the world in fishing. The sea around the islands of Japan furnishes octopi and seaweed for food for the Japanese.

Children draw and cut out fish of different sizes from paper. Attach a paper clip to the head of the fish and place it into a container. Tie a string to a magnet with a small hole in the middle and use as a fishing line to "fish" for carp, tuna or salmon.

Dissect Fish

Some children dissect fish or cut them apart to make a detailed examination. Place fish on a board. Make a slit with a knife from anus to head in order to expose the stomach cavity. Cut away rib section. Use a picture or drawing to tell the children the names of the organs. Children may draw an outline of a fish on a paper. Remove organs from fish and place them in the appropriate place on the diagram of the fish. Label the organs of the fish with words. Remember to inspect the craw to see what the fish had for supper.

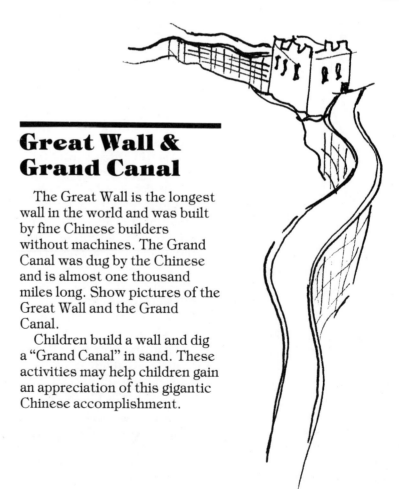

Great Wall & Grand Canal

The Great Wall is the longest wall in the world and was built by fine Chinese builders without machines. The Grand Canal was dug by the Chinese and is almost one thousand miles long. Show pictures of the Great Wall and the Grand Canal.

Children build a wall and dig a "Grand Canal" in sand. These activities may help children gain an appreciation of this gigantic Chinese accomplishment.

LANGUAGE DEVELOPMENT

Vocabulary

The following words are used to label pictures and objects made by the children:

bean sprouts — Japanese food.

clog — shoe with wooden sole worn out-of-doors.

dragon — a legendary fierce animal used in many Asian folktales.

futon — (foo TAHN) Japanese bedding.

geta — (GA tah) Japanese sandal.

hashi — (HAH she) chopsticks, special sticks for eating, used in Asian countries.

kimono — (kuh MOE no) a loose outer garment or type of dress, held in place by a sash and worn by Japanese men and women.

obi — (O bee) wide sash worn around waist, over kimono.

origami — (or ee GAH me) method of folding paper in Asian countries.

pagoda — (pah GO dah) temple with many stories which form a tower.

rice — grain of plant grown in warm climate of Asian countries, used for food.

shokki — (SHO kee) dishes for food, such as cups, bowls, plates.

tatami — (tah TAH mee) woven straw mat to cover the floor in a Japanese home.

tea — popular drink in Asian countries.

yew — (YU) fish.

Many pictures and books are available to acquaint the young child with the Asian cultures. New knowledge of interest to children encourages new language. Body language is important in the Asian cultures. Bowing is a way of communicating. It is the Japanese way of being polite and of showing respect for the other person.

Japanese Words Used in Conversation

sayonara — (sahy o NAHR ah) goodbye

konnichi wa — (kon NE che wah) hello

oahyo — (o HAH yo) good morning

arigato — (ah re GAH to) thank you

dozo — (DO zo) please

son — Mr., Mrs., Miss. Added to adult names, like, Alan-son

chan — added to child's name, like Jan-chan

Japanese Numbers

ichi — (i che) one
ni — (ne) two
san — (sun) three
shi — (she) four
go — five
roku — (rock u) six
shichi — (hich e) seven
hachi — (hach`e) eight
ku — (co) nine
ju — (jo) ten

Chinese Words Used in Conversation

Ni hao — (nee how) How are you?
hsieh hsieh ni — (shee shee nee) thank you
tsai chien — (tsigh jen) goodbye
ching — (cheeng) please

Chinese Numbers

i — (ee) one
erh — (er) two
san — (sahn) three
sze — (tsuh) four
wu — (woo) five
lui — (lyou) six
chi — (chee) seven
ba — (bah) eight
ju — (jew) nine
shih — (shirk) ten

Dramatization

After the children know a story and enjoy it, plan a dramatization of it with the children. Through asking them questions, have the children decide the characters and props or equipment which they need. The children act out the roles of the characters using the dialogue as they remember it. They will say the dialogue in their own words and with their own interpretation.

Favorite stories for dramatization:
- UMBRELLA
- ISSUN BOSHI: THE INCHLINGS
- TARO AND THE BAMBOO SHOOT
- THE DRAGON LIKED SMOKED FISH

Stories

The literature of a country or region of the world expresses the culture of that country. Stories, especially those written by authors who are natives of that country, provide authentic information about the culture. Stories are powerful sources of vocabulary and language development. They also provide many ideas for creative expression.

Storytime "happens" several times a day. A child brings a book, asks an adult to read it almost immediately; or he selects a book from the library or the book center in the room. The book is often read to one child or to a small group of children. At times, all of the children are interested in the same story.

Folktales

Adults in America expose young children to folktales and fairy tales. Some adults prefer to wait until the children are older. Each adult has to make a personal decision as to "when" it is appropriate to introduce folktales to children.

To expose children to folktales is to give them an insight into the thinking of a culture. The folktale is the clearest form of the beliefs of a culture. Young children become familiar with folktales through listening and dramatizing these tales.

Developmental stages of young children that make the enjoyment of folktales possible are a belief in magic, the lack of ability to separate real from make-believe in stories, a developing imagination, and an understanding of language.

Haiku

The art of creating Haiku is a gift from the Japanese culture. The poem has meaning for young children. Haiku has a definite pattern. It is a poem of three lines. The first line has five syllables, the second line has seven syllables and the third line has five syllables. Encourage three words for the first line. All children will not be interested in creating Haiku.

Haiku written by children at the Learning Tree—

Little curly dog
I saw him born yesterday
He likes people too.

Dog smelling flowers
Brown and curly is he so
A boy saw him go.

A horse smells flowers
Big and gray and big white ones
Feels soft and warm too.

Symbols

Use books, pictures and posters, to introduce children to Japanese and Chinese characters or letters. These characters, that look like pictures, are their alphabet. Each character is a whole word or idea. Several books in the bibliography include characters from both countries. Some children will copy them or use them as labels.

Many Japanese people write words in columns from top to bottom and from right to left. Children use a large piece of paper to apply bold brush strokes to make the symbols or characters. Black sticks of ink, Chinese Black, can be purchased at Asian shops.

Father

Mother

Boy

Girl

Tree

MUSIC AND DANCE

Music has a unique quality which is very different from western music. Sound is produced by flutes, drums, cymbals, lutes, gongs, wooden blocks and the samisen—a three-stringed instrument similar to the banjo.

Make available as many of these instruments as possible. Check local import shops. Children create their own music and imitate Japanese tunes.

Plum rains in early summer inspire songs about rain.

- JAPANESE RAIN SONG
- SPRINGTIME IS COMING
- CHI CHI PAPA

EMPRESS OF THE POGODAS is a song for listening and interpretive dance. The song may inspire children to create stories and poems.

GAMES AND MANIPULATIVE

Counting Game

Jan Ken Pon—a counting game used to pick the person who will be "it". Chanting "jan ken pon", two players shake fists up and down three times and then stretch their fingers out at the same time. Five fingers stretched out is paper, two is scissors, clenched fist is stone. If one player is paper and the other scissors, scissors wins because it cuts paper. If the two players are scissors and stone, stone wins because it can break scissors. If two players are paper and stone, paper wins because it can wrap itself around stone. If both players bring hands down in same position, they repeat game. The loser becomes "it".

Baseball
(Beisu bora)

Baseball is a very favorite sport in Japan. Young children dramatize this game. Try it without ball and bat! This activity allows children to learn the rules of the game.

Relay Games

Relay games are popular in Japan. Divide the children into two teams. The children in each team pass the ball from one child to another as fast as they can. First team to finish wins.

Additional Games

In and Out the Window is a popular game in Japan. It is also a singing game in America.

Ohajiki—(o hah JE ke) Marbles

SPECIAL EVENTS

Interest Trips

- Trip to Japanese gardens. Ohana mi, the experience of viewing and of listening to flowers is a sport in Japan. Locate a Japanese garden in your community.

- Trip to museum to view Japanese and Chinese art exhibits. Check your local museum and newspaper for Asian art exhibits.

Resource Persons

Invite a Japanese family to visit school to share culture. Include food, clothing, games, and stories and poetry. Possible menu:

- roast chicken (yake meshi)
- rice crackers (sembei)
- candies
- green tea
- mandarin oranges

Children gain insight from resource persons, interest trips and outings.

Japanese Calendar

Jan.	正月	New Year's Day.
	お正月料理	New Year's Dishes.
Feb.	豆撒き	Beans Throwing Ceremony.
Mar.	摘草 つみくさ	Gathering Young Herbs.
Apr.	桜祭	Cherry Blossom Fun.
May	五月節句	Boy's Day.
June	汐干狩	Digging for Shells.
July	七夕祭	Star Festival.
Aug.	しゃぼん玉遊び	Blowing Soap Bubbles.
Sept.	運動会	Sports Day.
Oct.	秋祭	Autumn Festival.
Nov.	かくれんぼ	Playing Hide and Seek.
Dec.	雪だるま	Making A Snowman.

Festivals in China and Japan

China and Japan are countries of many festivals. Find out which festivals are celebrated by the Chinese Americans and Japanese Americans in your region. Display pictures and books, and show slides and films of these festivals. Children dramatize these festivals, dance to the music, cook some of the special foods, try to be an acrobat and interpret the festivals with their creative expressions.

Japanese Festivals

New Year Day Festival
(O-Sho-Gatsu)

The New Year Day festival is a popular holiday. Banners are displayed. Families dress in kimonos and in traditional styles of clothing. Children and adults fly kites. Acrobats give a performance for the community.

The Japanese Americans celebrate New Year's day visiting each other. They serve the visitors traditional dishes; such as baked whole fish, gelatin squares of different colors and flavors, noodles and rice cakes. A sweet cake is served with the meal. The decorations are very symbolic. They include the lobster, symbol of old age; the tangerine, which means from generation to generation; and pine, symbol of endurance.

A game for New Year is hanetsuki. It is similar to badminton. It is played with a hagoita—a paddle, and a birdie.

"Songs of a Hundred Poets" is a game played only during this season. The game is similar to the game of American Authors.

To adapt this game for young children, use a regular deck of cards. Select pairs of cards from the deck, about four pairs for each player. Deal all the cards. Dealer begins game by calling for a card that matches one in his hand. Each player in turn calls for a card. The game is over when all the cards are paired. The winner is the one who holds the most pairs of cards. After children learn the game, they suggest many variations.

Doll Festival
(O Hina Sama)
March 3

Girls dress in kimonos and kneel on cushions. They eat rice cakes and candies. Dolls and blossoms of early spring flowers are displayed.

On this day and for many days, the Japanese Young Women's Christian Association in San Francisco, displays a collection of O-hina dolls.

Hana Matsure—Japanese American Festival. April 9 (date changes)

The Japanese Americans in San Francisco combine several Japanese festivals on this day. On the first Sunday the cherry trees are in bloom, they gather at the Japanese tea garden in Golden Gate Park for a celebration.

Boy's Day, May 5

Boy's Day is celebrated by flying a giant paper carp banner. The carp is the symbol of power and strength. The carp banner is flown from a long bamboo pole in front of Japanese homes, one fish for each son in the family. Boys display dolls of warriors in armor and famous Japanese heroes who represent strength and bravery. Instructions for making a carp banner are in the section on Creative Art in this chapter.

Star Festival, July 7

The traditional offerings for this festival are stories and poems written by the Japanese; and they eat slices of peaches and melons. They decorate the room with bamboo and cherry blossoms. Instructions for making paper flowers are in the chapter on Mexican Cultures in this book.

Chinese and Chinese-American Festivals

Chinese New Year (Yuan Tan). Date varies from January 21 to February 19.

New Year is a happy holiday for the Chinese. The date changes each year because the Chinese use the lunar calendar. Their New Year is celebrated on the first day of the lunar calendar. Americans use the solar calendar. The Chinese begin their celebration with a family dinner. It includes fish because it is a symbol of prosperity. Homes are decorated with red because this color is a symbol of happiness to all Chinese. The Chinese celebrate with a parade and music, followed by fireworks.

New Year's Day is the biggest celebration for the Chinese in Chinatown in America. It is a day when debts are paid, accounts settled, and grudges are forgotten. The celebration includes fireworks; a dragon dance through the streets of Chinatown; beating of drums, gongs and cymbals; and wonderful special foods for this holiday.

Spring Festival, April 2-5

The Spring festival is a Chinese American holiday. The Chinese honor the planting season in this celebration.

The Dragon Boat Festival, Fifth day of the fifth month of the Chinese calendar

This festival is very picturesque. The celebration includes boat races with boats shaped like a dragon.

Moon Festival, September 15-16

A harvest festival which honors the autumn moon. It is a woman's festival and is celebrated at night. The moon festival is similar to the Thanksgiving holiday in America. This Chinese harvest festival is celebrated by Chinese Americans.

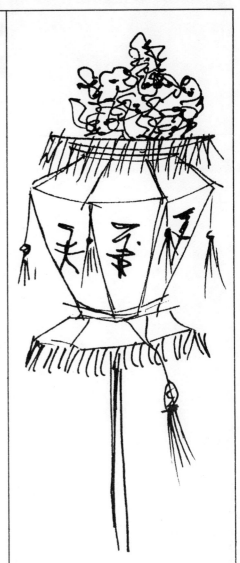

Chinese May Day, October 1

Chinese children perform acrobatics; and they dance, fly banners and show their animals or crops on this day. Many Chinese families attend the fireworks display in the evening.

Winter Festival, December 21 (date changes)

The Winter festival is celebrated entirely within the family. No public displays are held. The festival is usually held a few days before the Christmas holidays in America. Some Chinese Americans celebrate this festival.

SELECTED BIBLIOGRAPHY

Asian American Cultures

Books for Children

Anno, Mitsumasa. **Anno's Alphabet: An Adventure in Imagination**. Crowell, 1975.

Creative presentation of letters and objects by a Japanesed artist.

Asian Cultural Center for UNESCO, **Stories from Asia Today**, Weatherhill, 1980.

A collection of stories for young readers and young listeners.

Atwood, Ann. **Haiku: The Mood of the Earth**. Scribner's, 1971.

Numerous color photographs and words promote an experience in an appreciation of nature.

Ayer, Jacqueline, **Nu Dang and His Kite**, Harcourt, Brace and Jovanovich, 1972.

Kites are popular pastimes in Asian countries.

Balaban, John, tr., **Vietnamese Folk Poetry**, Unicorn, 1974.
To know the poetry of a culture.

Batterberry, Michael. **Chinese and Oriental Art**. McGraw-Hill, 1961.

A book for browsing. Handsome photographs of prints and oriental art forms.

Behn, Harry, **More Cricket Songs**, Harcourt, Brace and Javonich, 1971.

Reading Haiku, illustrated by Japanese artists, often leads to children's writing and illustrating of their own haiku. Same author also wrote **Cricket Songs**.

Coutant, Helen. **First Snow**. Knopf, 1974.

Warm, sensitive drawings and text examine a Vietnamese American girl's search for the meaning of death.

Edelman, Lily. **Japan in Story and Pictures**. Harcourt, Brace and World, 1953.

Festival days—kite flying, cardplaying (karcita). Doll party with glimpses of kimonos and dolls.

Forney, E.H. and Inor, **Our Friends in Viet-nam**, Tuttle, 1967.

Booklet portrays the Vietnamese, the attractive friendly and brave people that some are. Many black and white line drawings are authentic.

The Beautiful Princess
ISSUN BOSHI

BY LORI

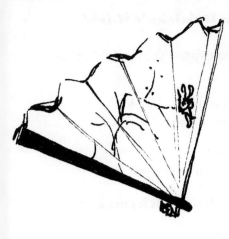

Glubok, Shirley. **The Art of China**. Macmillian, 1973.

    Author is early childhood educator. Text with photographs for young readers. Survey of art.

Glubok, Shirley. **The Art of Japan.** Macmillian, 1970.

    An introduction to Japanese painting, sculpture, flower arrangements and gardens. Suggests painting a great wave similar to Kokusai.

Iwasaki, Chikiro. **What's Fun Without a Friend?** McGraw-Hill, 1975.

    A story about understanding between two children. Books by Iwasaki children enjoy are **A New Baby Is Coming, The Birthday Wish** and **Will You Be My Friend?**

Matsuno, Masako. **Taro and the Bamboo Shoot.** Pantheon Books, 1974.

    Young boy's adventures in a bamboo grove. Japanese folktale; excellent for dramatizing. Yasuo Segawa's illustrations increase interest in the tale.

Mosele, Arlene. **The Funny Little Woman**. Dutton, 1972.

    Children delight in the "scary" illustrations and the adventures of the little woman and the wicked one.

Mosel, Arlene. **Tikki Tikki Tembo**. Holt, Rinehart & Winston, 1968.

    Young children are the wise ones in this humorous tale about why Chinese names are short.

Nigaha, Kuzuo. **Clouds**. Addison-Wesley, 1975.

    Japanese artists of numerous children's books reflections of clouds.

Phillips, Barbara. **Noy Noy and the Charcoal Man.** Addison-Wesley, 1970.

    An adventure that captures the culture of Thailand with story about boiled rice and spice for breakfast, the clattering coal wagon, sweet smelling papayas in brimming baskets swaying from a pole, a sweet coffee and tea vendor, banana trees, a Seklu selling colored beads and a fried noodle vendor.

Robertson, Dorothy Lewis, retold. **Fairy Tales from Vietnam**. Dodd, Mead, 1968.

    Stories of talking animals and magic should be selectively read or told to young children.

Sarasas, Claude. **The ABS's of Origami: Paper Folding for Children**. Tuttle, 1964.

    Origami projects made simple by descriptive diagrams and illustrations. Some young children engage in this activity without difficulty.

Soong, Maying. **The Art of Chinese Paper Folding: For Young and Old**. New York: Harcourt, Brace & World, 1948.

    Clear instructions and simple diagrams for paper folding.

Sterberg, Martha. **Japan: A Week in Daisicke's World**. MacMillian, 1973.

Full-page photographs of Minoru Aoki expose young children to both modern and traditional Japan.

Tabrah, Ruth ed., **Issuboshi**, Island Heritage, 1974.

Folktale of Japan. Good story for dramatizing.

Tamara, ST., **Asian Crafts**, Lion, 1972.

Instructions for making crafts from Asian countries.

Wyndham, Robert. **Chinese Mother Goose Rhymes**. World, 1968.

Art of creating haikus is an oriental gift to the world. These three-line expressions are meaningful to young children as they create their own poems.

Yashima, Taro. **Crow Boy**. Viking Press, 1955.

Yashima takes us on a search of valuable truths. Helps children see value in understanding the feelings of others.

Yahima, Mitsu and Taro. **Momo's Kitten**. Viking Press, 1961.

Momo's experience with kitten has value for young children who are making discoveries about growth and reproduction.

Yashima, Taro. **Seashore Story**. Viking, 1967.

A tale about Urashima, the fisherman, who went on a journey to the bottom of the ocean and "stayed away too long".

Yashima, Taro. **Umbrella**. Viking Press, 1969.

Japanese-American Momo desires to use new gifts which can only be used on rainy days. Three-year-old learns patience and self-confidence.

Yashima, Taro. **The Village Tree**. Viking, 1953.

A tree for climbing, swinging, see-sawing, a chair, a house, a place for a snack, or a game of "Bamboo-Hide". Full of activities that appeal to children, one of Yashima's best.

The children at the Learning Tree also enjoy these books. Look in your library for them.

Baron, Virginia O. ed., **The Seasons of Time: Tanka Poetry of Ancient Japan.**

Baron, Virginia O., **Sunset in a Spider Web: Sijo Poetry of Ancient Korea.**

Berger, Donald P., **Folk Songs of Japanese Children Songs from Japan.**

Bryant, Sara C., **The Burning Rice Fields.**

Cassidy, Sylvia and K. Saetake, **Birds, Frogs and Moonlight.**

Copeland, Helen. **Meet Miki Takino.**

Hirawa, Yasuko, **Song of the Sour Plum: And Other Japanese Children's Songs.**

Herman, Ralph, **Lee Lan Flies the Dragon Kite.**

Ishii, Momoko, **Issunboshi: The Inchlings.**

Issa, Yayu, **Kikaku and other Japanese poets, don't tell the scarecrow and other Japanese poems.**

Larson, Joan P., **Visit With Us in Japan.**

Lewis, Thomas P., **The Dragon Kite.**

Matsuno, Masako, **A Pair of Red Clogs.**

Mezumiua, Kazue, **I See the Winds.**

Miller, Richard J. and L. Katol, **Japan.**

Otsuha, Yuzo, **Suko and the White Horse: A Legend of Mongolia.**

Pitts, Forrest R., **Japan.**

Pratt, Davis and E. Kula, **Animals of Japan.**

Titus, Eve, **The Two Stonecutters.**

Weise, Kurt, **You Can Write Chinese.**

White, Florence and K. Akiyama, **Children's Songs from Japan.**

Wiens, Herold T., **China.**

Yashima, Mitsu and T., **Plenty to Watch.**

Yashima, Taro, **Youngest One.**

Zimelman, Nathan, **A Good Morning's Work.**

Books for Adults

Adams, William, ed., **Asian-American Authors**, Houghton Mifflin, 1972.
  Bibliographical sketches and photograph of each author, with an example of his writing. Useful for helping children identify with models.

Buell, Hal. **Viet Nam: Land of Many Dragons**. Dodd, Mead, 1968.
  Resource for teacher. Excellent photographs of the Vietnamese people engaged in planting and cultivation of rice, and fishing in Mekong Delta's marshland.

Chinese Bilingual Pilot Project, San Francisco United School District, 135 Van Ness Avenue, San Francisco, CA 94102.
  Materials for children, developed for this project. Request list of publications.

Daniels, Roger, **Asian Experiences in North America: Chinese and Japanese**, Arno, 1979.
  Describes the life of these cultures in America. All experiences have not been happy ones.

Davidson, Georgie, **Origami**, Larousse, 1978.
  Once children understand the basic paper folding techniques, the step-by-step instructions and the illustrations with each of the 136 figures, they can use this book by themselves. Figures of Japanese paper folding are arranged from simple to more difficult.

Dunn, Lynn P., **Asian Americans: A Study Guide and Resourcebook,** R & E, 1975.

Brief outline for learning the history of Chinese, Japanese, Koreans, Filipinos and other Asian cultures who came to America. Additional references.

Gage, William and D.T. Binh, **Vietnamese-English Phrase Book With Useful Word List: For English Speakers**, 1975, Center for Applied Linguistics, 3520 Prospect Street NW, Washington, DC 20007.

Used for learning some Vietnamese words and for translating when Vietnamese come to your school.

Hundley Jr., Norris ed., **The Asian American: The Historical Experience**, 1976. American Bibliographic Center, Cleo Press Inc., 2040 Alameda Padre Sierra, Santa Barbara, CA 93103.

Separate chapters on the Chinese, Japanese, Filipinos, Koreans and East Indian communities. Historical sketch about each Asian culture.

Japanese American Curriculum Project, P.O. Box 367, San Mateo, CA 94401.

A distribution center for English and bilingual materials about Asian Americans for children and adults. Excellent source for educators.

Martinello, Marian L. and W. T. Field, **Who Are the Chinese Texans?** 1979. Institute of Texan Cultures, 801 South Bowie Street, San Antonio, TX 78205.

Photographs with text—history of the Chinese in Texas to the present day. Good description of culture and their contributions.

Melendy, H. Brett, **Asians in America, Filipinos, Koreans and East Indians**, Twayne, 1977.

Helps reader realize that many Asian cultures live in America.

National Indochinese Clearinghouse, Center for Applied Linguistics, ERIC Clearinghouse for Language and Linguistics, 3520 Prospect Street NW, Washington, DC 20007.

Materials for working with children and families from Indochina, especially Vietnamese and Thais. Preschool level included. Helps for cultural understanding and learning English as a second language.

Sung, Betty L., **Album of Chinese Americans**, Watts, 1977.

Serve as real models for Asian American children. All children need to know that all Americans contributed to our country.

Thuy, Vuong G., **Getting to Know the Vietnamese and Their Culture**, Ungar, 1976.

Helpful for understanding the culture of the Vietnamese who have come to America in recent years.

Wolff, Diane, **Chinese Writing**, an introduction, Holt, Rinehart & Winston, 1975.

Some children copy Chinese characters and compare them to the ABC's.

Magazines

Bridge Quarterly
Basement Workshop Inc., 199 Lafayette Street, New York, NY 10012

Small magazine, edited by and for, young people. Goal is to "bridge" Western and Asian cultures. Emphasis is on young Asian American students, especially as expressed in their poetry, art and short prose.

Japan Quarterly
Japan National Tourist Organization, 45 Rockefeller Plaza, New York, NY 10020

Illustrates in large colorful photographs, the developments in Japan, the interests of modern Japan and a glimpse of the traditional culture. In English.

Korea Journal Monthly
Korea National Commission for UNESCO, C.P.O. Box 64, South Korea

Devoted to arts, music, drama, folklore and history of Korea.

Free China Review Monthly
Chinese Information Service, 159 Lexington Avenue, New York, NY 10016

News about culture, special events, science and education in Taiwan and China.

Records and Film

"Chi Chi Pa Pa" with Margaret Marks. **Making Music Your Own.** Album 6 records. Silver Burdett Company. Dist: General Learning Corporation, 8301 Ambassador Road, Dallas, Texas 75247. Album 75180.

Have you ever heard about a school for birds? This song tells about one.

"Empress of the Pagodas: **Making Music Your Own**. Album 6 records. Silver Burdett Company. Dist: GEneral Learning Corporation, 8301 Ambassador Road, Dallas, Texas 75247. Album 75180.

Asian sound, listening music. Children create and dramatize stories.

"Festival in Japan", American-English version. Sakura Motion Picture Company, Ltd. Dist: Japan National Tourist Organization, 45 Rockefeller Plaza, New York, NY 10020. Film 67, 21 minutes.

"Japan In Winter", American-English version. Sakura Motion Picture Company, Ltd. Dist: Japan National Tourist Organization, 45 Rockefeller Plaza, New York, NY 10020. Film 46, 17 minutes.

Scenes with birds migrating, kite flying, farming, fishing, ice skating. Entertaining for young children.

"Japanese Rain Song" with Roberta McLaughlin. **Making Music Your Own.** Album 6 records. Silver Burdett Company. Dist: General Learning Corporation, 8301 Ambassador Album 75180.

A rainy day in Japan prompts gestures and movement.

Black Cultures

Black American African Heritage

Africa is a country of varied regions and many cultures; and, it is far away. Generally, it is not appropriate for young children to study about a country or place they cannot visit. However, the African heritage is important to some Black American families. Also, an understanding of the African heritage can help all cultures understand the influence of African traditions on the American cultures. Caribbean and Latin American Black cultures are not included in this book. The contributions of some Black Americans are included. You can add the names of many more Black Americans from your region who have made important contributions to America.

Children need to understand the differences between the African people who lived long ago and the way the African cultures live today.

FAMILY LIVING

African Village

When the environment is changed into an African village, young children role play the life of the village. The role playing activity is a way to make the experience meaningful to children.

The following suggestions are ways to prepare the classroom environment for an African experience.

The way people live in Africa depends upon the region in which they live. The adults prepare the classroom environment, allowing children opportunities to extend the experience with their own ideas.

The Family Living Center is the basis of cultural awareness of the American experiences. How families live, what they eat, what they wear and how they care for their babies can be explored in this center. Children extend the ideas they begin in the home center with activities from other learning centers in the room.

By John

Homes

A tree house on stilts in the classroom provides an African home. Green bamboo sticks, long enough to wedge between the floor and ceiling, are placed in the room and around the home or the tree house to give the effect of a jungle.

A large cardboard carton can be used for a home. Windows and doors can be cut. Children can paint the sides in earth tones. Dried grass can be piled on the top to give an appearance of an authentic Zulu home.

Furnishings

The following items are furnished to encourage role playing the home life of one of the numerous African groups. Adults and children can make them. Instructions for making them are in this section.

straw baskets — woven straw baskets are used to carry on heads or to serve peanuts and fruits.

clothing — dashikis, kentes and kerchiefs for children.

calabash — a drinking vessel made from a calabash gourd.

masks — carved wooden masks are available at import stores and worn by children.

jewelry — bead necklaces, bracelets, earrings or the jewelry made by children.

mesh bags -- Some African mothers use loosely woven cloth bags to carry their babies. A strap of cloth is attached to the sides of the bag and the mother places this strap on her head and the bag hangs in front of her. Boys and girls use this method to carry their dolls. Mesh potato or fruit sacks can be used.

Clothing

Headdress

Headdresses are an important part of a costume when a successor to the chief is selected, as a district ruler over several village chiefs or as a young prince dancing in preparation for becoming a royal page.

To make a "banana fiber" ceremonial headdress, a child can decorate a 12" x 18" piece of colored construction paper. Fringe and staple to form a crown effect. To fringe, draw a line across one long side of the paper approximately two inches from the edge. Cut slits vertically from the other long side to that line. Colored feathers, yarn and colored paper glued to the headdress give a special effect.

Kente (KEN-te)

The kente is a sarong type dress or toga worn by men and women of various tribes in Africa. It is the national dress of Ghana and is made from brightly-colored handwoven cloth. This wrap-cloth dress is wrapped around the body and tied in a knot on one shoulder.

Use 1 yard x 2 yards piece of fabric. Some children will want to decorate the kente with colorful designs. To wear, hold one corner to one shoulder. Wrap kente around the body under the arm. Tie two corners together on one shoulder.

The art of painting is learned by children. Place a wet paper towel in a shallow dish. Sprinkle with small amount of dry tempera. Children press a

gadget (spool, bottle top, block, potato masher) into the tempera paint, and paint a design on construction paper or cotton fabric used for kente.

Dance Skirt

Raffia or grass dance skirts are worn by some Africans in ceremonial dances.

To make, use two folded sheets of newspaper, full-size sheets. Place a strip of fabric between the newspaper at fold. Fringe in long slits up to 1 inch of fold. Gather skirt on strip of fabric and tie around waist.

Kerchief

A head scarf is worn by African women in many tribes to market and as part of formal festive dress. Some scarves are decorated elaborately and others are plain. This style is used by many Black American women today.

Children can make a kerchief that ties around the forehead or at the nape of the neck to cover hair. Decorate a 16" x 28" x 16" triangle of fabric using markers or crayons. THE CLEVER TURTLE has good examples of African print.

Dashiki (de-SHE-ke)

The dashiki, a ceremonial shirt worn by some African men, has become fashionable in America for men, women and children. This shirt is made from colorful patterned fabric.

Fold a 12" x 36" piece of old sheet or fabric. Cut a hole for the neck large enough to fit over the child's head. The sides are open. The child can decorate the dashiki with crayons and felt markers. It can be worn with or without a sash.

Fabric printed for making dashikis can be purchased at fabric stores. The fabric has beautiful designs and colors. Teachers or parents can make several child-size dashikis to be worn by the children in their role playing activities.

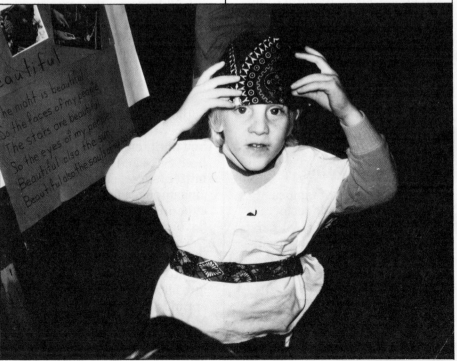

Foods and Cooking Experiences

Foods differ in various regions. However, common foods in most areas are corn (mealie is a common mush), cassava (tapioca), yams and bananas. Any experience that involves taste adds another one of the senses. Using as many senses as possible, helps the young child understand an idea or concept.

Tapioca

Tapioca Fruit Soup

2 tablespoons quick-cooking tapioca
1½ cups water
1 tablespoon sugar
dash of salt
½ cup quick-frozen concentrated orange juice
½ cup diced orange sections
1 medium banana diced

Combine the tapioca and water in saucepan. Cook and stir over medium heat until mixture comes to a boil. Remove from heat. Add sugar, salt and orange juice. Stir to blend. Cool, stirring after 15 minutes. Cover and chill. Fold in orange sections and sliced bananas. Other fruits may be substituted.

Tapioca Pudding

Buy packages of tapioca. Child or adult reads recipe. Children can measure, stir and make all preparations. Discuss how tapioca comes from cassava root. Some children may write or dictate what they did.

Yams

Yams or sweet potatoes are grown in many sections of Africa. They are basic food for many African families.

Children peel the raw yams, put in a pan and cover with water. Boil in salted water until tender. Drain. Add sugar and butter. Have children mash them, then eat them.

Yams can also be cooked without peeling. Place in a pan, cover with water, add salt, and boil until tender. Drain, cool, peel. Slice and serve. Have butter, sugar, salt, pepper and cinnamon available to experiment with different flavors.

The yams can also be fried as french-fries. Allow one-half potato per child. Peel and cut into slices. After frying, sprinkle with sugar.

Peanut Stew

Peanut stew can be made from raw or roasted peanuts. Roasted peanuts give a better flavor. Children enjoy shelling the peanuts.

Combine:

1 cup roasted shelled peanuts
4 cups water
5 beef bouillon cubes

Bring to boil. Then simmer for 15 minutes. Add salt to taste. Serve hot or cold.

Chocolate Pudding

Mix in cup:
2 tablespoons instant chocolate
　　pudding
1/3 cup cold milk

Stir until thick.

An African Beverage

Milk and Honey

The African custom is to make this drink in a large trough made from a hollowed log. All of the people drink from this trough with long reed straws. Each child will enjoy drinking through a straw in the African style.

Mix:
1 cup honey
½ gallon cold milk

Pour into a shallow pan. Drink with drinking straws.

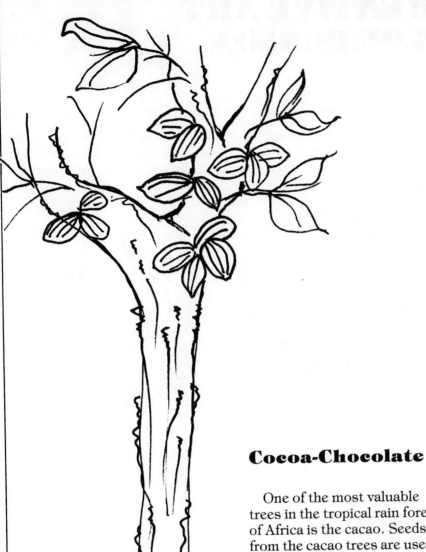

Cocoa-Chocolate

One of the most valuable trees in the tropical rain forests of Africa is the cacao. Seeds from the cacao trees are used to make cocoa and chocolate. In the book, THE DRUMS SPEAK, brilliant pictures depict the gathering of cocoa in Africa.

Peanut Butter

1½ cups salted roasted
　　peanuts
1 tablespoon oil

Put peanuts and oil into blender and blend to the desired consistency. One tablespoon of honey may be added for flavor. Let children spread on crackers or bread.

Provide several different forms of chocolate for tasting.

- powdered cocoa
- unsweetened chocolate
- chocolate candy bar
- instant chocolate pudding

Extend this tasting experience by preparing hot chocolate and chocolate pudding. Children make their own serving.

Hot Chocolate

Mix in cup:
1 teaspoon cocoa
3 teaspoons sugar
1/3 cup powdered milk

Fill cup with hot water. Stir. Children enjoy measuring, stirring and drinking their own hot chocolate. Some children are surprised that sugar has to be added to chocolate to sweeten it.

Fried Bananas

To fry bananas, children slice bananas length-wise. Sprinkle with lemon juice, brown sugar and cinnamon. Fry in small amount of butter.

CREATIVE ART EXPRESSION

Jewelry

The creativity of some Africans is demonstrated in the way they use bone, shell, stone and metal to make necklaces, bracelets, earrings and rings. This heavy jewelry is worn on arms, legs and necks by some of the African tribes. Children can make all kinds of jewelry if appropriate materials, interesting books and descriptive pictures are available to them.

Rings

Rings can be made by wrapping a fine wire around a finger several times. Children find a small "special" stone. They wrap the end of the piece of wire around the stone several times to attach it to the ring. Spools of fine wire in silver or gold finish can be purchased at variety stores.

Necklaces and Bracelets

Necklaces and bracelets are made by stringing shells, animal bones and nuts such as acorns and pecans. Use yarn, inexpensive leather strips or colored electrical wire for stringing. Department stores carry packages of small drill bits that can be used for piercing holes. Colored wire is available from a telephone company. Leather strips can be purchased in quantity at sporting goods stores.

Masai Collar Necklaces

Circles of metal wire hang from the Masai woman's neck and hang over her entire chest.

The necklaces are so heavy and hot that special leaves are placed between the skin and ornaments to soothe the skin.

Use a large paper plate. Cut out the center of the paper plate. Children can decorate the rim of the plate with designs. Punch holes in the rim and hang shells and clay beads off the outer edge of the rim with wire. Cut the rim in one place and fit around the child's neck.

Clay Beads

Mix:

1 cup cornstarch
1½ cups soda
1 cup cold water

Cook until thick and until it pulls away from sides of pan. Stir frequently. Children form small marble-sized beads from the clay. Make a hole in each bead with a toothpick. Bake 45 minutes at 300 degrees.

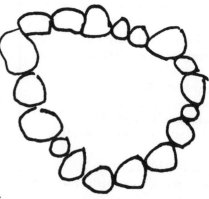

Charcoal Drawings

Some Africans use charcoal as a drawing tool. A partially burned log was brought to school, and the children made drawings with the pieces of the charcoal they had broken from the log. Later in the year, while on an outing, the children discovered an old campfire. Immediately, they asked for paper so they could draw with the charcoal they had found. The paper was given to the children and they extended an activity that they had experienced in the African culture earlier in the year.

Masks

African tribes use elaborately decorated masks. Masks are used with movement and music to celebrate life and to place control on the Spirits. Many cultures in Africa use masks in their dances.

Picture books of masks are included in the bibliography at the end of this chapter. Some children may not be interested in making masks. Make cardboard, construction paper and posterboard available. After children become familiar with different kinds of masks from the pictures, they cut the cardboard the desired size and shape for a mask. The children then select a variety of materials from the following: feathers, yarn, shells, clay, paint and metal disks. These materials are glued to the cardboard shape. Other features can be added with paint and crayons. Attach a piece of string or elastic to each side of the mask.

Children's creations vary because of their different developmental levels.

- Some children will use the materials to make collages.
- Some children will draw or paint a picture of a mask.
- Some children will create elaborate masks.

A display of wooden and papier-mâché masks and picture books helps children create masks.

Shields

Dazzling shields were once a part of a warrior's tribal war costume. Today Africans use shields in dances to act out the victories won by warriors in the past.

Children use ideas from pictures and books, talking about the ideas with other children.

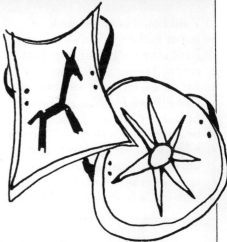

Provide materials, such as felt markers, crayons, leather strips, paints, fabric and brad fasteners. Use a 12" x 18" piece of cardboard the desired shape. Children decorate their shields selecting from the materials. Attach a strap for carrying. Each child decides where he will attach the strap, depending on how he wants to carry the shield.

Another way of making a shield: Children like to hunt for sticks to make a shield. Frames can be made by tying the sticks together. Willow sticks are easily bent and make good frames. Decorate a piece of paper the shape of the willow frame and attach to the frame. Attach a strap for carrying.

dancers, bowls and similar items.

•Children put several symbols or objects together. For example, they will create a mother and a baby and play with them together.

Pottery

Throughout the centuries Africans have recorded their history through their art. People all over the world have used African art forms. Some Africans still make pottery by hand. Today many Africans still use the ancient method to make dishes and other useful objects.

To make clay pottery pieces, use natural red clay or potter's clay. See the section on Creative Art Expression in the chapter on Native Americans for directions.

Dogon and Zula Houses

A small replica of Dogon and Zulu homes can be made of paper and clay. These houses have clay walls and thatched roofs. These can be made by forming a circular wall of clay. Cut straws from an old broom or use dry grass. Gather grass or straw into a bunch. Tie ends of grass or straw at one end with wire. Spread out other ends of grass or straw over the clay walls to make the thatched roof. A door can be drawn on the side of the clay wall with a sharp instrument.

Clay

Clay is explored by children according to their developmental stages.

•Children who are in the manipulative stage make clay ropes, snakes and pound clay into many shapes.

•Children who have moved into the next stage of development will create African

Black Artists

Children examine books, paintings, sculpture and pottery to gain an appreciation for the contributions of Black artists. Black artists include Benny Andrews, Cleveland Bellow, Vivian Browne, Norma Morgan, Paul Keene, Franklin White, Russ Thompson, Raymond Saunders.

NATURE AND SCIENCE

By John

Coconuts

Coconut palm trees grow in East Africa. The meat of coconuts is used as food and the milk is used as a drink. The fronds or branches from the palm tree are used to make thatched roofs. The oil from the dried coconut meat, called copra, is used in making soaps and cosmetics.

Coconuts can provide many learning experiences for young children. Children enjoy looking at them, feeling the surface and shaking the coconut to listen to the sound of the milk inside. This activity encourages many questions which are answered by using resource materials. Many times questions also lead the child to resources outside the classroom.

One way to open a coconut is to make a hole by hammering a nail into one eye. Children are eager to make this hole themselves. Some of the children want to taste the milk. Pour all of the milk out of the coconut. The coconut can then be placed on newspapers spread on the floor. A hammer can be used to break the coconut. Children take turns hitting the coconut until it breaks. As the children taste the meat of the coconut, they suggest appropriate words to describe the taste. Packaged coconut can be provided for children to taste and to compare with the fresh coconut.

Gourds

In some parts of Africa, gourds grow wild and the bottle-shaped fruits are dried and used to hold water and other liquids. One kind of gourd, called the calabash, with its hard tough shell, is used as a cooking pot over a fire. Other types of gourds are used in Africa as cups, bowls and for musical instruments; such as rattles and stringed instruments.

Children can do many things with gourds. Display a variety of dried gourds for children. They will shake them and guess what is inside the gourd. Cut one of them open to show the inside. Cut gourds in half and clean out the inside. Children can use these for cups. Save the seeds and plant them or string them to make jewelry. Some gourds can be used as rattles for creative sound in dancing.

Plant gourd seeds. Seeds may be planted in spring and allowed to mature on the vine. This takes several months depending upon the locality. The harvest may be used during the study of the African heritage.

Groundnuts

Groundnuts in Africa are the same as peanuts in America. A basket of groundnuts or peanuts could be provided for the children to count, crack and eat. Discuss how they grow and how they are harvested. Use pictures and resource materials. Take a trip to a peanut field.

LANGUAGE DEVELOPMENT

Language development is one way of becoming aware of other cultures. The "hands on" experiences involve talking to other children and adults, listening to stories and to new ideas and adding new words to their oral language. Real experiences give meaning to the new words. Sometimes the new words are the beginning of a second language. New experiences usually result in many questions as children try to understand the new cultures. The African environment in the classroom encourages thinking, exploring and asking questions.

Children are exposed to new words through the objects, pictures and artifacts in the room as well as through real experiences and creative activities. Many pictures and books about the African cultures help children learn new words as they become aware of the lifestyle of the cultures. As the children request labels for their activities, tell stories and engage in dramatic play, they use these new words. Each child will be interested in different words—the words that have a personal meaning for that individual child.

The following words are used in labeling pictures and objects in the room. This is a suggested list; other words may be added.

Swahili—(swa HE le) the language spoken throughout East Africa.

Bantu—(BAN tu) a tribe in South Africa.

Masai—(MA si) a tribe of tall natives of East Africa who raise cattle.

Watusi—(wah TU se) a tribe of people of Central Africa, many of whom are over seven feet tall.

Dogon—(DOH gohn) a tribe of cliff dwellers of West Africa.

Pygmy—(PIG mee) a tribe of people who live near the equator in Africa who are less than five feet tall.

Anansi—(ah NAN see) a character in a group of old African folktales; Anansi is part spider and part man.

Vocabulary

Swahili Words

karibu—(ka REE bu) welcome

rafiki—(rah FEE kee) friend

jambo—(JAM bo) hello

ngoma—(na GOL mah) drum and dance

fagio—(fah GEE o) broom

tembo—(TEM bo) elephant

punda—(POON dah) donkey

uzuri—(u ZOO ree) beauty

watoto—(wah TOE toe) children

chakula—(cha KOO la) food

gudulia—(goo DOO lee ah) clay jar

mama—(MAH mah) mother

baba—(BAH bah) father

Print words on cards for children who are printing. Some children are ready to print while others are not. Children will use some of these words in the stories they dictate to adults.

Africa
Congo
Atlantic
jungle
grassland
desert
equator
safari
groundnut
cassava
calabash
tattoo
kente
dashiki
dialect

Dramatization

Most often children provide props or items needed for their roles in dramatizing stories. Some children need other children or adults to assist them in locating props. Activities such as these encourage the adults to collect different materials to satisfy the spontaneous needs of children.

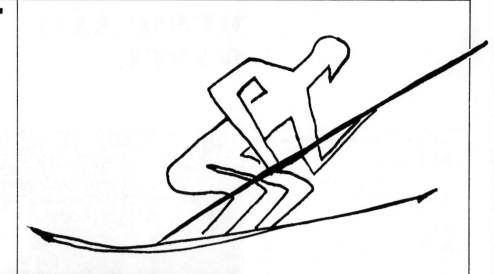

Folktales

Some adults expose young children to folktales from the African cultures while others wait until the children are older. Many adults in America tell folktales and fairy tales to young children. To expose children to folktales is to give them some understanding of how the people in a culture think. The folktale is the clearest form of the beliefs of a culture. Young children do not understand all the history, folklore and symbolic of a folktale. Neither can they understand it outside of the culture it describes. Early exposure to folktales can set a foundation for understanding more fully in later years. Young children enjoy the interesting characters, the predictable pattern of the story, the adventure, and the animals who talk and do what people do. Examples of folktales that young children enjoy hearing and dramatizing are:

• ANANSI, THE SPIDER: A TALE FROM THE ASHANTI
• A STORY, A STORY
• WHY THE SUN AND THE MOON LIVE IN THE SKY
• WHY THE SUN WAS LATE
• THE CLEVER TURTLE.

MUSIC AND DANCE

Dance

Dancing is important in African life because it is a way of self expression. When Africans dance together, they get to know each other, to feel each other and to relate to each other. West Africans sing as they walk with baskets on their heads. Movement is carried over into dances from the walking steps.

African Rhythms

African music is not written but handed down from person to person. Most musicians spend their entire lives perfecting their skill on native instruments. The musician takes a rhythmic pattern that he has been taught, but plays it in his own way. The Black people are known through the world for their ability to improvise. From the journal MAN AND HIS MUSIC. See bibliography.

Many Africans have a unique way of making music with their bodies.
- clapping hands
- slapping bodies, shoulders, sides and thighs with hands
- clicking tongues
- stomping feet

African rhythms are started by the adult. Children will imitate the pattern of the adult leader. First, without music, then adding the authentic African music. Children learn the rhythm very quickly and soon create their own rhythm patterns. Children and adults imitate the rhythm patterns created by each other.

Musical Instruments

The people in some countries in Africa use their natural resources to make musical instruments. If possible, instruments used in Africa or similar ones should be available for use by the children.

African String Instruments

A type of guitar with goat skin stretched over a wooden frame with wire strings. Available at some import shops. When Arabic people came to Africa they brought string instruments. The oud (ood) a form of lute, lyre, simple harps and fiddles were the most popular.

Bongo Drums

Available in import and music stores.

Wooden Xylophone

Make from eight ½" x 2" boards. The longest board is 12" long. Sand and shellac the boards and place them on 2" x 16" strips of carpet. Strike the boards with a wooden mallet for an unusual musical tone. Young children can measure tone.

Drums

Drums are made from tree trunks, elephant tusks and clay. These drums are covered with the hides of native animals.

A drum for the classroom is a large solid plastic leaf basket turned upside-down. The sound is beautiful. Children strike the basket with their hands. Several children can play the drum at the same time. Tall plastic waste baskets make a different sound. Experiment with different kinds of baskets.

Some drums the children make:
•drums from cans and large ice cream containers.
•arm drums made from oatmeal boxes, carried by some Africans under their arms while dancing or parading.

Flutes

Africans make flutes of different lengths. Each length makes a different tone. Flutes can be made from cardboard tubes, toilet tissue tubes, paper towel tubes and wrapping paper tubes.

Rattlers

Rattlers are made from tin cans or cardboard juice cans containing a few pebbles or dried beans. Cover open end.

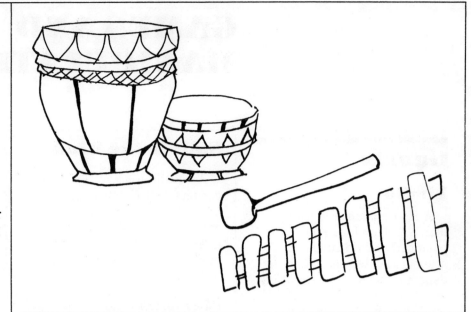

Songs
Jazz

In African music there is often a leader who sings a solo line and a chorus of singers that answer. It is this kind of response singing brought by the Blacks from Africa that led to the call-and-answer type of singing in American Negro spirituals and later jazz. American jazz is popular throughout much of Africa. From MAN AND HIS MUSIC— See bibliography.

Music by Black artists— Aretha Franklin and Stevie Wonder are Black artists who express the basic African rhythms in their music.

Records

LITTLE JOHNNY BROWN by Ella Jenkins. A collection of songs that have been passed down for generations in Black communities throughout the United States. Includes songs, chants, and civil rights freedom songs.

RHYTHMS OF CHILDHOOD—AFRICAN IMPRESSIONS, by Ella Jenkins. A collection of authentic African chants and folksongs. These chants encourage interpretive dance.

A RAM SAM SAM— MAKING MUSIC YOUR OWN record album. An African folk song. Children enjoy dancing to this rhythm.

Books

MUSICAL INSTRUMENTS OF AFRICA is an excellent resource for adults. This book helps them to gain knowledge and an understanding of music and rhythms of Africa. This book provides information about the musical instruments, the dances and the different body rhythms and movements used by African dancers. A record accompanies this book.

Interpretation of Poetry

Children enjoy the poetry of Langston Hughes. They create interpretive dance to "Danse Africaine" and "The Night is Beautiful" from the book SELECTED POEMS by L. Hughes.

GAMES AND MANIPULATIVES

Games

Limbo

A Haitian dance. Children dance under a long stick balanced on two chairs. The stick is lowered each time the dancer dances under the stick without touching the stick. The winner is the one who can dance under the lowest position of the stick, without touching it.

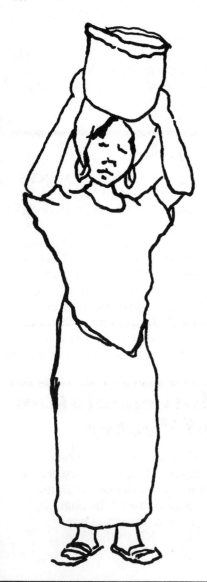

Sails in the Wind

An outdoor game. Tie two corners of 36" x 36" silk scarf around a child's waist as if you were making a skirt. The child holds the other two corners in his hands and sails by running in the wind.

Marbles

African and American children play similar games. Some of these games are hopscotch, marbles, soccer, jacks, one potato, two potato, jump rope, and duck, duck, goose.

Marbles can be played by shooting nuts, pecans, hickory nuts or acorns with the thumb. The target is other nuts placed in a circle on the floor or outdoors on the ground.

Manipulatives

- View Master with reels of Africa.
- Puzzles of African wild animals.
- Black dolls from Shindana Toys, 4161 South Central, Los Angeles, CA 90011.

Basket Balancing

Africans carry heavy loads on their heads. The children imitate the adults by balancing small straw baskets on their heads while walking across the room.

SPECIAL EVENTS

Black Artists

Local Black American dancers, painters, sculptors and musicians come to school to share their Black culture through each art form. They communicate to the children through music, dance and creative handcrafts. In the African cultures, the dance brings people together as a tribe and the tribe is important to the stability of African cultures. Black American dancers demonstrate dances from the African and Black American cultures. They explain and show basic African movement to young children.

Take a trip to the art museum to see African art exhibits. Ask for special guide for young children.

Holidays

Emancipation Day

September 22
This is the anniversary of the day that Lincoln read the Emancipation Proclamation in 1862.

Harambee Day

Last week in October
During the week prior to Halloween some communities observe "Harambee Day" which means "Let's all pull together".

Zawadi

December 26 through January 1
To recognize the traditional African harvest festivals some Black families celebrate Christmas by sharing small homemade gifts, Zawadi. A community-wide feast is held on the last day and African foods, songs and dances are shared by the families.

Emancipation Proclamation
(Afro-American)

January 1
Anniversary of the signing of the Emancipation Proclamation by President Lincoln freeing the slaves.

National Freedom Day

February 1
This day is set aside to commemorate the signing by President Abraham Lincoln of the proclamation of abolition of slavery, 1863.

National Black History Week

Second week in February

Soul Food Dinner

Black parents prepare and offer soul food to children and adults. Menu might include:

Turnip Greens or Collards
Red Beans
Rice
Sweet Potato Pie
Chitt'lins
Blackeyed Peas
Cornbread
Banana Pudding

Chitt'lins

Chitterlings from one young
   hog (10 pounds)
1 tablespoon salt
1 tablespoon pepper
1 red pepper, chopped
1 tablespoon whole cloves

Wash chitterlings 5 or 6 times. Trim fat, leaving some for flavor. Cover with salted boiling water. Add cloves and red pepper. Cook until tender. Drain and cut in pieces. Dip each piece in egg batter then cracker crumbs. Deep fry until brown.

Collard Greens

2 pounds chicken neckbones
4 bunches collard greens
2 tablespoons bacon drippings
salt and pepper
dash of Tabasco sauce

Parboil neckbones until tender, remove from pot. Add well-washed greens that have been chopped. Cook over low flame until greens are done. Add bacon fat and season to taste. Greens should be cooked uncovered and almost at a full boil so that you end up with only a small amount of "likker". This can be poured over the greens before serving.

Red Beans

Wash 2 cups dried pinto beans. Cover the beans with three inches of cold water and cook. Add salt pork, ham hock or bacon drippings. Bring to rapid boil. Reduce heat and simmer 1 to 3 hours, or until tender. Add hot water as needed as cold water bursts beans. Stir from bottom as needed. Serves 8.

Roast Corn Cobs

5 earns corn
½ cup soft margarine
1 teaspoon salt
½ teaspoon paprika
dash of pepper
dash of Tabasco sauce

Pull husks away from corn but do not tear off. Remove the corn silk. Spread the corn with mixture of margarine, salt, paprika, pepper and hot pepper sauce. Fold husks over cob. Wrap the corn in foil. Bake at 375 degrees for ½ hour in oven or cook over moderately hot coals in a barbecue grill.

Banana Pudding

¾ cup sugar
1/3 cup flour
¼ teaspoon salt
2 cups milk
2 eggs, separated
1 teaspoon vanilla
36 vanilla wafers
3 medium bananas, sliced

Blend ½ cup sugar, flour and salt thoroughly together in top of double boiler. Add ½ cup milk, stirring to make smooth. Add remaining milk. Cook over boiling water, stirring frequently until thickened. Cover, cool 15 minutes. Beat egg yolks slightly, add hot custard slowly to yolks. Return to double boiler, cook 2 minutes. Remove from heat, add vanilla. Line bottom and sides of a baking dish, 6" x 10" x 2", with wafers. Beat egg whites stiff; add remaining sugar, spread over pudding, and bake at 325 degrees for 20 minutes.

Corn Fritters

1 cup flour
1 teaspoon baking powder
½ teaspoon salt
¼ cup milk
1 egg
1 teaspoon butter
1 cup drained crushed corn

Mix the dry ingredients, gradually adding the milk and the well-beaten egg. Beat thoroughly and then add the melted butter and corn. Drop by the spoonful into hot deep fat and fry until brown. Drain on paper towels.

Short'nin Bread

4 cups flour
1 cup light brown sugar
1 pound melted butter

Mix flour and sugar. Add butter. Place on floured surface and pat to ½ inch thickness. Cut into desired shapes and bake in moderate oven (325-350 degrees) for 20-25 minutes.

Cornbread

1 cup yellow corn meal
1 cup sifted all-purpose flour
¼ cup sugar
4 teaspoons baking powder

½ teaspoon salt
1 egg
1 cup milk
¼ cup shortening, soft

Sift together corn meal, flour, sugar, baking powder and salt into bowl. Add egg, milk and shortening. Beat with rotary beater until smooth, about 1 minute. Bake in greased 8-inch square baking pan in pre-heated hot oven (425 degrees) for 20-25 minutes.

SELECTED BIBLIOGRAPHY

Black American Cultures

By Shelley

Books for Children

Aardema, Verna, retold. **Behind the Back of the Mountain: Black Folktales from Southern Africa.** Dial Press, 1973.

Leo and Diane Dillion, illustrators, join with author in relating folktales from Africa.

Aardema, Verna, retold. **Why Mosquitoles Buzz in Peoples' Ears**. Dial Press, 1975.

A West African tale about a disaster caused when Mosquito tells Iguana a "tall tale." Cleverly told by Aardema and brilliantly illustrated by Leo and Diane Dillion. Watercolor/airbrush illustrations.

Adoff, Arnold, ed. **Black Out Loud: An Anthology of Modern Poems by Black Americans**. MacMillan, 1970.

Brave poets—Langston Hughes, Le Roi Jones, Nikki Giovanni, and Gwendolyn Brooks convey Black pride.

Adoff, Arnold, ed. **My Black Me: A Beginning Book of Black Poetry**. Dutton, 1975.

Represents the thoughts of poets, Nikki Giovanni, Langston Hughes and others.

Alkema, Chester. **Masks**. Sterling, 1971.

Vividly illustrated book showing witch doctors, animals and a "do do" spirit. Suggestions creating a mask.

Allen, William D. **Africa and South America**. Fideler, 1978.

Resource book with full-page photographs of villages, people and animals of Africa that can be used in preparing the environment to arouse the curiosity of young children.

Baldwin, Anne. **Sunflowers for Tina**. Four Winds Press, 1970.

Bold colors and descriptive text portray a sensitive Black child's feelings about life and death. Positive Black imagery.

Bernheim, Marc and Evelyn. **African Success Story: The Ivory Coast**. Harcourt, Brace and World, Inc., 1970.

Information and vivid photographs of Savanna villages, cocoa trees and African people.

Bernheim, Marc and Evelyn. **The Drums Speak: Story of Kozi, a Boy of West Africa**. Harcourt Brace Javanovich, 1971.

Book of photographs with lengthy text depicts life-style in West African village where life changes very slowly. Section on cocoa harvest.

Bernheim, Marc and Evelyn. **A Week in Aya's World: The Ivory Coast**, MacMillan, 1969.

Aya, in Africa, visits animals at the zoo, plays Blind Man's Bluff, pounds yams in a wooden mortar and sleeps on the floor. Suggests similarities and differences from American lifestyle.

Breinburg, Petronella. **Dr. Shawn**. Crowell, 1975.

Shawn, a Black child, is leader of children playing "hospital." Suggests girls may be doctors.

Breinburg, Petronella. **Shawn Goes to School**. Crowell, 1973.

Children identify with the first day at school when "Shawn didn't like it very much."

Clifton, Lucille. **The Boy Who Didn't Believe in Spring.** Dutton, 1973.

The author, an authority on Black dialect, has captured Black-American language. Depicts an integrated school and community with Black majority. Available in Spanish.

Clifton, Lucille. **Don't You Remember?** Dutton, 1973. Two

Two famous Black artists, Evaline Ness illustrator, portray a positive Black family image.

D'Amato, Alex and Janet. **African Crafts for You to Make**. Julian Messner, Inc., 1970.

Directions on how to make replicas of chad houses, tie-die fabrics and the game "manhala".

Dayrell, Elphinstone. **Why the Sun and the Moon Live in the Sky**. Houghton Mifflin, 1968.

African folktale about the origin of the world.

Desbarats, Peter. **Gabriella and Selena**. Harcourt Brace Jovanovich, 1968.

A story of a relationship between a Black child and a White child.

Dietz, Betty, and A. and M. Babatunde, **Musical Instruments of Africa**. John Day, 1965.

About the many instruments used by Africans to accompany their music. Ideas for making instrument with "whatever material is at hand". Record accompanies book. Points out how Africa has inspired music in America.

Elisofon, Eliot. **Zaire: A Week in Joseph's World**. Crowell-Collier Press, 1973.

Joseph Mohobi's life in central Africa. Pictures of fish market, hippos playing and a game of soccer played by boys with bare feet on wet ground.

Feelings, Muriel. **Jambo Means Hello**. Dial Press, 1974.

Swahili alphabet book. For language and cultural information.

By Melissa

By Melissa

Feelings, Muriel. **Moja Means One: Swahili Counting Book**. Dial Press, 1971.

One to ten in Swahili. Describes East African cultural traits. Illustrations of market stalls, mothers, instruments, manhala and coffee trees.

Fraser, Kathleen and M. F. Levy. **Adam's World: San Francisco**. Whitman, 1971.

Positive family relations. Full-page illustrations. How one Black community lives, and where Black pride is reflected.

Glubok, Shirley. **The Art of Africa**. Harper & Row, 1965.

Photographs of masks, headdresses, neck rests and gold weights. Descriptive text of interest to young children.

Graham, Lorenz. **Song of the Boat**. Crowell, 1975.

Momolu searches for a canoe for his beloved father. Authenticity revealed in style and content; poetic style shows rhythm of the language. Woodcut by Lee and Diane Willion.

Greenfield, Eloise. **First Pink Light**. Crowell, 1976.

Concerned about his ill mother, Tyree waits for his father's return. Soft charcoal illustrations enhance warmth of story.

Greenfield, Eloise. **Me and Nessie**. Crowell, 1975.

Nessie has an imaginary friend: Her Black family deals with the situation in a sensitive way.

Haley, Gail E. **A Story, A Story: An African Tale Retold**. Atheneum, 1970.

Adventures of Ananse, the "Spider Man" as he outwits others in order to pay the price that Sky God wants for stories. Geometric illustrations in bold colors. Suggests that African myths may have inspired folklore, proverbs and moral stories in other cultures.

Hoffman, Phyllis. **Steffie and Me**. Harper & Row, 1970.

Day in the life of an advantaged young girl.

Hopkins, Lee B., ed. **Don't You Turn Back: Poems by Langston Hughes**. Knopf, 1967.

A collection of poems selected by young children for a poetry memorial. Includes "Mother to Son" and "Dream Variations."

Hughes, Langston. **First Book of Africa**. Franklin Watts, 1960.

From ancient Africa to Africa today. Illustrated with photographs. Coffee trees, gold mines and section on children of Africa.

Hughes, Langston. **Selected Poems.** Knopf, 1971.

Hughes' poems foster expressions in dance and painting.

Hunt, Kari, and B. Carlson. "Masks of Africa", **Masks & Mask Makers**. Abingdon Press, 1961, pp. 34-39.

Illustrations and brief text show how masks play an important part in Africa's rituals.

Jones, Bessie, and B.L. Harris. **Step It Down**. Harper & Row, 1972.

Songs and games for children from the Black cultures. Moves from learning "how to clap" to the sophisticated rhythms. Excellent.

Keats, Ezra. **Goggles**. Macmillan, 1969.

Adventure of three friends and their struggle over a pair of goggles. Delightful illustrations.

Keats, Ezra. **Hi Cat**. Macmillan, 1970.

A hilarious tale about Archie planning a show. Humorous illustrations.

Lexau, Joan M. **Benjie**. Dial Press, 1964.

A terrible incident turned bashful Benjie into a boy who "hadn't let anybody stop him from finding the earring."

Lexau, Joan M. **Benjie On His Own**. Dial Press, 1970.

Author and illustrator, Don Bolognese, join in a story about isolation, poverty and kindness that exist together in a community.

McDermott, Gerald. **Anansi, The Spider: A Tale From the Ashanti**. Holt, Rinehart & Winston, 1972.

This story from Ghana, passed on orally for many generations. Illustrations of geometric forms and colors.

McGovern, Ann. **Black is Beautiful**. Four Winds Press, 1972.
Positive black imagery leads to appreciation by all children.

Mendoza, George. **And I Must Hurry for the Sea Is Coming In.** Prentice-Hall, 1969. Photographs by DeWayne Dalrymple.

Black child dreams of the sea. Brief poem accompanies text.

Pine, Tillie S., and J. Levine. **The Africans Knew**. McGraw-Hill, 1967.

Each tribe of Africans used the things around them to help them in their daily life. Ideas for making things.

Roberts, Nancy. **A Week in Robert's World: The South**. MacMillan, 1969.
Robert Lee's world is a supporting, caring and interesting one.

Schatz, Letta. **Benji's Magic Wheel**. Follett, 1975.

A teacher in Nigeria tells a story about growing up in a West African village. Ann Grifalcone's woodcuts are expressive.

Scott, Ann Herbert. **Sam**. McGraw-Hill, 1967.

Sam needs someone in his family but all are busy until Sam makes his need known. Illustrations by Symeon Shimin of beautiful Black family.

Steptoe, John. **Stevie**. Harper & Row, 1969.

About how a child feels when he is confronted with sharing toys, mothers and homes. Realistic city environment.

By Karch

Sutherland, Efua. **Playtime in Africa**. Atheneum, 1963.
Games and pastime reaction are written in poetic form.

Thomas, Ianthe. **Lordy Aunt Hattie**. Harper & Row, 1973.

Black author writes the mood and feeling of early summertime in Black dialect. Quiet pictures and rhythmic text.

Wagner, Jane. **J.T.** Dell, 1971, Film from Miller Brody.

Based on true life of a ghetto child in an integrated neighborhood. Problems in racism, sexism and inadequate ways of dealing with death. Film is a consciousness-raising experience for parents. Evaluate whether or not to use it with children.

The children at the Learning Tree also enjoy the following books. Look for them in your library.

Clifton, Lucille, **Good, Says Jerome**

Crippen, David, **Two Sides of the River**

Elkin, Benjamin, **Why the Sun Was Late**

Foster, F. Blanche, **Dahomey**

Gray, Genevieve, **Send Wendell**

Hodges, Elizabeth J., **Free As A Frog**

Kalibala, Ernest B. and M. G. Davis, **Wakaima and the Clay Man and Other African Folktales**

Klimowieg, Barbara, **When Shoes Eat Socks**

Marshall, Anthony D., **Africa's Living Arts**

Mason, Robert G., **The Life Picture Book of Animals**

Roche, A.K., **The Clever Turtle**

Seed, Jenny, **Kulimi the Brave: A Zulu Tale**

Stone, Elberta, **I'm Glad I'm Me**

By Karen

Books for Adults

Carey, Willie, M., **Worse Than Silence: The Black Child's Dilemma**. Vantage Press, 1978.

A book on the problems of the inner city Black child with suggestions for improving conditions for these children.

Coleman, Madeleine, ed., **Black Children Just Keep on Growing**. 1977, Black Child Development Institute, 1463 Rhode Island NW, Washington, DC 20005.

Describes Black programs for children from the 1960's with summary of learning tasks which appeared consistently in the programs. Also a review of literature by Black researchers on topics relating to the Black child.

Comer, James P. and A. F. Poussaint, **Black Child Care**. Simon and Schuster, 1975.

Authors are Black psychiatrists from Yale and Harvard who explain how to bring up a healthy Black child in America.

Crane, Louise. **The Land and People of the Congo**. Lippincott, 1971.

Facts about the land, people and culture of the Congo. Good section on art and music.

Curriculum Approaches From a Black Perspective. 1973, Black Child Development Institute, 1463 Rhode Island Avenue, NW, Washington, DC 20005.

Book of readings. Reflect wide variety of experiences about Black child's learning.

Driskell, David C., **Two Centuries of Black American Art**. Knopf, 1976.

Traces Black American art. Work of 63 artists. Art includes paintings, sculpture, graphics, crafts, dolls, and walking sticks.

Dunn, Lynn P., **Black Americans**; a study guide and sourcebook. R & E Associates, 1975.

A beginning study of history from 1400 to 1975 of the Black experience in America. Many references listed.

Harrison-Ross, Phyllis and B. Wyden, **The Black Child**. Wyden, 1973.

Raises the consciousness on the unconscious ways we teach racial prejudice to children from the day they are born.

Latimer, Bettye, I., ed. **Starting Out Right: Choosing Books About Black People for Young Children**. 1972.

Provides a conceptual framework for children's books dealing with Black Americans by offering guidelines and rationale for examining this new body of literature.

Lewis, Francione N., **Selecting Children's Books with a Black Perspective,** 1975, Far West Laboratory for Educational Research and Development, 1855 Folsom Street, San Francisco, CA 94103.

Guide to analyze materials about Black Americans. Topics deal with reality in Black life and historical accuracy.

MacCann, Donnarae, and G. Woodard. **The Black American in Books for Children: Readings in Racism**. Scarecrow Press, 1972.

Examples of racism in popular books. Guidelines for criteria for self-evaluation.

McLaughlin, Clara J. and others, **The Black Parents' Handbook**, Harcourt Brace Jovanovich, 1976.

Special needs of caring for Black children and the differences in development as compared to White children.

Ojigbo, A. Okion, ed. **Young and Black in Africa**. Random House, 1971.

Insight about growing up in Africa.

Shockley, Anna. and S. P. Chandler, eds. **Living Black American Authors**, Bowker, 1973.

Acquaint children with living Black American authors in all fields of work.

Spodek, Bernard, **A Black Studies Curriculum for Early Childhood Education**, revised edition, Black Studies Curriculum Development Project, Catalog #150, ERIC/ECE, University of Illinois, 805 West Pennsylvania Avenue, Urbana, IL 61801.

Presents in outline form the objectives, content, teaching procedures and materials for four units: A Look at Africa, Language Experiences Through Black Media, Afro-American arts and Social Studies.

Thum, Marcella, **Exploring Black America**, a history and guide, Atheneum, 1975.

Provides the missing pages in history books. Information and photographs include Black historic sites and landmarks, museums, pioneers and cowboys, artists and craftsmen, storytellers, musicians, scholars—Black Americans through the years.

Magazines

Man and His Music (Special issue on "Africa", January, 1973). Quarterly. Keyboard Jr. Publications, 1346 Chapel Street, New Haven, CO 16511.

For children ages 5 through 12. All art forms are explored, especially music.

Ebony Monthly
Johnson Publishing Company Inc., 820 Michigan Avenue, Chicago, IL 60605.

Many photographs of the successes of Black life and cultures. National and international events and news of the Black cultures. Excellent for colored pictures and models of Black Americans.

Ebony Jr! Ten issues a year.
Jefferson Publishing Company, address above.

"Reflects the sound and sights and colors of your Black community." Stimulates pride in Black history. For children up to age 12. Includes games, stories, Black personalities, history, events, recipes, and arts and crafts. Book reviews and calendar of important events.

Golden Legacy Five issues a year.
Fitzgerald Publishing Company Inc., 527 Madison Avenue, New York, NY 10022.

Black history is presented in comic magazine form. Written so young people can understand and appreciate Black history. Authentic information. Includes Black Americans, literature and study of ancient African kingdoms.

Records and Films

"African Noel", **Making Music Your Own**. Album 6 records. Silver Burdett Company. Dist: General Learning Corporation, 8301 Ambassador Road, Dallas, Texas 75247. Album 75180.

This Liberian folksong is brief and young children learn the lyrics easily.

"A Ram Sam Sam", **Making Music Your Own**. Album 6 records. Silver Burdett Company. Album 75180.

This folk song from Africa involves children in movement and in singing the African lyrics. Book accompanies album.

The Black Experience in Children's Audiovisual Materials, 1973, Office of Children's Services, New York Public Library, The Branch Libraries, 8 East 40 Street, New York, NY 10016.

Annotated list of records and cassettes, films, filmstrips and multimedia kits. Many were produced for adults but they are also useful with children.

Caldmon Records, 404 Eighth Avenue, New York, NY 10018.

Catalog lists new record releases and categorizes by age. Numerous folktales.

Ethnic Dances of Black People Around the World with Marie Brooks. Kimbo Educational Records. Distributed by Educational Activities, P.O. Box 392, Freeport, NY 11520. Album #11520.

Manual will enable adults to create steps for use with children. Possibilities for creative and interpretive movement.

Little Johnny Brown, with Ella Jenkins. 1 record. Prod: Folkways Records. Dist: Scholastic Records, 906 Sylvan Avenue, Englewood Cliffs, New Jersey 07632. Record SC7631

Collection of songs which has been sung in the Black community for generations. The songs which children like to sing are: "Little Johnny Brown", "Hammer, Hammer, Hammer," "Miss Mary Mack", "He's Got the Whole World in His Hands", and "Freedom Train".

"Rhythms of Far Away", **Rhythms of Childhood**, with Ella Jenkins. 1 record. Folkway Records. Dist: Scholastic Records. Address above. Record SC7653.

Freedom and work chants from Africa. "Kum Ba Ya", a spiritual from Liberia in West Africa will be familiar to some children. "Come By Here" (Kum Ba Ya) is easily learned by young children. "En Komo Zee Gah Ba Ba" (My Father a Cattle) is a cattle-herding song.

Children's Book and Music Center
5373 West Pico Blvd., Los Angeles, CA 90019.

Write for catalog. Source for recordings and books.

Posters and Pictures

Black ABC's: **Picture Story Prints**. Society for Visual Education, Inc., 1345 Diversey Parkway, Chicago, Illinois 60614.

Alphabet posters (26 prints in color) with emphasis on Black culture are valuable for use with all children.

Dolls

Shindana Toys, 4161 S. Central, Los Angeles, California 90011.

Dolls and games with Black and Afro-American context. Catalog is available.

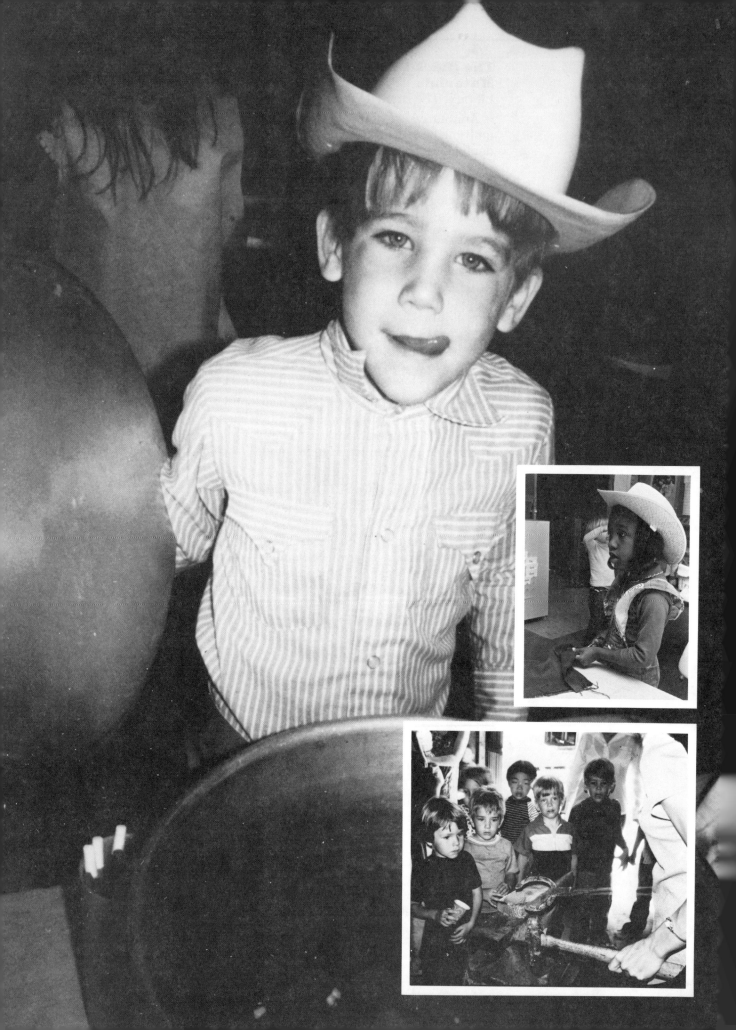

Cowboy Culture

Pioneers and Early Texans

The excitement of the cowboy adventures, past and present—cattle drives, roundups, branding the animals, camping out, cooking over an open fire and riding in a rodeo, is an adventure for young children.

Many of the cowboy activities have been modernized. However, on some of the cattle ranches in the United States today, the work is still performed in the same ways that they were in the middle 1800's.

The children at the Learning Tree have the opportunity to extend cowboy life to other western cultures. They explore pioneer family life at the same time.

FAMILY LIVING

Furnishings

The prepared environment for outdoor living for cowboys includes:

bedrolls — made from animal skins, quilts or large bath towels.

campfire — a "campfire" built of logs stacked in crisscross fashion in a central area. Children gather around the "campfire" to sing cowboy songs, to share "wild tales" or to pretend to cook.

cots — a canvas cot.

lean-to — a tarpaulin made of canvas, stretched across an area, makes a shelter large enough to spread bedrolls.

water keg — a large container that looks like a fifty-gallon keg, filled with drinking water.

metal cups — cups made from tin cans, opened so there are no sharp edges, used to dip a cool drink of water from the keg.

angle iron — a metal triangle used to call cowboys to meals — use a rhythm band triangle.

utensils — wooden bowls, spoons, metal pots, pans, coffee pot and plates for camping.

chairs — logs sawed in about 1 to 2-foot lengths, also camp stools.

bale of hay — adds to the western atmosphere.

sawhorses — "bronco busters" ride the wooden sawhorses.

The working life-style of the cowboy was unique. The job of rounding up cattle and moving them from ranches where they were raised, to the nearest railroad involved the cowboy in an adventure apart from his family. The cowgirl imitates this adventurous westerner.

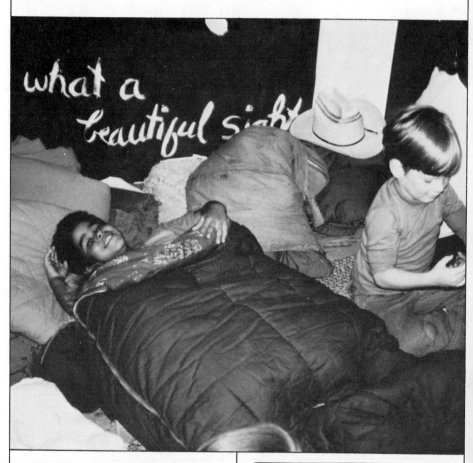

wooden spool horse — a wooden cable spool makes a horse large enough for several children. Cable spools are available from telephone or power companies.

saddle — an authentic leather saddle strapped to the wooden spool horse.

lasso — ropes may be tied to fence posts, around rocks and horses' heads. Supervise this activity carefully.

Clothing

Cowboy clothing includes:

- aprons, bonnets and long skirts
- bandana handkerchiefs
- boots
- chaps
- hats
- leather gloves
- leather vests
- spurs

To discourage the violence children see in movies about cowboys, provide a place for hanging guns when children enter the indoor work area. Children are encouraged to use the guns **ONLY** for "killing snakes and wild varmints".

Foods and Cooking Experiences

In the early days the meals for the cowboys were cooked over an open fire. The kind and quality of food depended upon the ability of the person who was hired as the cook for the roundup or the cattle drive.

"Come and get it" meant coming together to eat beans, boiled potatoes, stew, gravy, stewed fruit, and sometimes ribs and steak.

Food, stored in a box, looks like the small cupboard that the roundup cook used at the back end of the chuck wagon.

The following foods were popular with the cowboys.

"Spuds"
Potatoes

Peel and slice potatoes. Cover with water. Cook until tender. Drain, butter and eat. One-half potato serves one child.

"Son-of-a-Gun in a sack"
Pudding in a Sack

Make individual servings of instant pudding. Mix in cup 2 tablespoons instant pudding with 1/3 cup cold milk. Stir until thick. Put into small plastic bags.

"Shivering Liz"

Any food that has the quivering quality of jelly. Make jello. Two large packages of jello serves twenty children.

"Lick"
Molasses

Make a hole in the top of a biscuit. Fill the hole with molasses or syrup.

"Air Tights"
Canned Food

Any canned food, such as pork and beans or corn.

Pinto Beans

Dried pinto beans were popular with the cowboy. Have children wash beans, put them into a large pot, cover with water, season with a strip of bacon and salt. Cook until tender, about 2½ hours.

"Spotted Pup"

Cook rice and raisins together. Add ½ cup raisins to 2 cups of rice. Cook according to directions on package. This amount serves twenty children.

Cowboy Sweet Rolls

Use hot roll mix. Prepare according to directions on package. Sprinkle with cinnamon and brown sugar. Bake.

Roundup Stew

4 pounds hamburger
10 poltatoes
2 pounds carrots
3 onions
2 bunches celery
2 large cans tomatoes
2 small cans corn
2 small cans cut green beans
3 cups water
salt and pepper

Salt and pepper the meat. Make small meat balls. Fry in electric skillet until brown. Peel potatoes, carrots and onions and cut into small chunks. Add chopped celery. Open canned foods and pour into large pot. Add other vegetables, meat balls and water. Add salt and pepper to taste. Cook 1½ hours at medium heat. Serves about 35.

Cornmeal

Children make their own cornmeal. Husk dried ears of

corn. Pound the kernels to break them from cob. Use a blender to crush the kernels. This cornmeal will be like coarse flour. Use this meal in hoecake, a version of the familiar cornbread.

Hoecake

2 cups cornmeal
1 teaspoon salt
boiling water

Mix cornmeal and salt. Add boiling water, enough to make a thick batter. Spread 1 heaping tablespoon of batter in hot, greased frying pan. Cook until brown on one side, turn and cook on other side. Butter and eat.

Sour-Dough Biscuits

1 cup milk
1 teaspoon salt
1 heaping teaspoon baking powder
1 heaping tablespoon shortening
2½ cups flour

Mix milk, salt, baking powder and shortening. Add flour. Stir until mixed. Each child kneads a small amount of dough on floured wax paper. Flatten dough and cut biscuits with a small fruit can. Roll biscuits in melted shortening. Place them close together in a large bread pan. Bake at 450 degrees until brown, about 10 minutes. Butter and eat.

Some children carry an extra biscuit in their "ditty bag" while they are on the cattle drive.

Wild Game Rabbit

Cowboy and pioneer families ate wild game for meat. Rabbits which are raised for eating can be purchased from rabbit farms. Prepare rabbit by cutting it into pieces. Children flour and salt the pieces of rabbit. Adult places them in hot oil in a skillet. Fry until tender.

Chicken

Domestic animals were raised for food by the pioneer families. Fry chicken, using same method as for rabbit.

Wild Pigs

Strips of meat were often smoked over the fire. Fry salt pork or bacon.

Pioneer families prepared these foods:

Roasting Ears — Clean husk and silk from ear of corn. Place in a pot of boiling water. Boil ten minutes. Pour off the water. Butter, salt and eat.

Corn — Buy and eat cans of creamed and whole kernel corn.

Popcorn — Prepare popcorn. Learning Tree wranglers eat popcorn around the campfire.

CREATIVE ART EXPRESSION

Clothing

The style of clothing of the cowboy changed after the cattle business was established on the plains. Cowboy dress became more distinctive.

Children "rig up" in cowboy garb—chaps, vests, rope belts, neckerchief and spurs. Adults make basic clothing. Children decorate the clothing with leather strings.

Vests

Sleeveless vests were worn by cowboys instead of coats because the cowboys could move their arms easier without sleeves.

Cut vests from plastic wall covering. Punch holes in underarm sides. Lace underarm sides together with yarn or leather strips. Add a pocket to the vest with brad fasteners. Adapt the size of the pattern to each child.

Neckerchief

A bandana worn around the neck is a good mask for protection from dust or it can be used as a pouch to carry articles.

Make the neckerchief from gingham fabric. Cut triangular pieces of fabric 12" x 18" x 12".

Chaps

The word "chap" came from the Spanish word "chaparreras". Chaps are leather leg-coverings worn by the cowboy to protect his legs from thorny brush.

Make chaps from plastic wall covering purchased at department stores. Cut a band long enough to fit around the child's hips and add enough length so the chaps can be tied in the back. Cut two large pieces for leg-coverings. Attach leg-coverings to the band with brad fasteners. Attach two leather strings to each side of each leg-covering. Tie in back of knee. Fringe outer edge of leg-coverings. Chaps can also be made from heavy brown paper. Adjust pattern to size of child.

Spurs

Spurs are sharp metal prongs strapped to the cowboy's boots to help him control his horse. The decoration on the spur identified the cowboy's home. Sometimes bells and chains were fastened to the spur.

Make spurs by fastening bottle caps to a leather or heavy cloth strip with wire. Punch a hole in bottle cap with a hammer and nail. Thread wire through the hole and attach the cap to the center of a 1" x 12" leather strip. Tie this "spur" around lower ankle, over the boot or shoe with bottle cap "rowel" at the back of the heel.

Belts

Young children find more pleasure in wearing belts made from rope than cowboys did.

One-yard lengths of small jute rope make belts which are tied around the waist and knotted in the front.

Slicker

A slicker was a cape that usually was yellow and served as protection from the rain and cold. Cowboys tied and carried their slicker behind the saddle.

Use a paper cape for a slicker. Cut cape from heavy brown paper about 36" x 36". Plastic drop cloth can be used. Attach yarn strings to each side and tie around neck. Children delight in wearing capes and playing the role of a cowboy.

Ditty Bag

Ditty bags, sometimes called "warbags", were used as a storage place for personal belongings; such as a shirt, socks, letters or a catalog. The cowboy rolled the bag into his bedroll when he traveled. Sometimes the cowboy carried a sour-dough biscuit or a piece of jerky in his ditty bag for snacks along the trail.

Bags can be made from 8" x 12" pieces of fabric. Fold the fabric in the center and sew along two sides, leaving the top open. Some children, who can manage a needle, can sew the sides together. Make holes an inch apart around the top edge. Lace yarn or leather string through the holes to make a drawstring bag. Use pieces cut off of jeans for ditty bags.

Scarf Ring

A ring is worn to hold neckerchief in place.

Rings are made from empty toilet tissue rolls. Three rings can be cut from one roll. Decorate them by drawing brands on sides of ring, using felt markers. Pull ends of scarf through the rings.

Cuffs

Leather gauntlets were worn by some cowboys to protect their wrists and shirt sleeves from thorny brush. These cuffs were sometimes decorated with metal nail heads called studs.

Make cuffs from 5" x 8" pieces of plastic wall covering. Decorate the cuffs with studs made from different sizes of brad fasteners. Wrap the cuffs around the wrist. Fasten ends together with brads.

Cup Tree

Cups are hung on a cup tree. The tree is made by hammering nails into a four-foot 1" x 12" board. Hang on the wall at a height young children can reach.

Tin Cup

A tin cup was used by the cowboy for drinking coffee or for eating stew.
Make tin cups by wrapping a 10" length of wire around the top of a small tin can. Twist ends of wire into a loop to make a handle. Print names on cups.

Brands

A mark burned on the side of a horse or cow shows who owns the animals. A display of brands and a branding iron will encourage children to create their own brands.

This symbol is carved into a soft piece of wood with a nail or drawn on a square of styrofoam with a pencil. Use styrofoam meat trays, cut in half. The piece of styrofoam or wood can be tacked to a two-foot long stick. Apply thin tempera mixture to the surface and paint the brand on paper, vests, chaps and ditty bags.

Rattlesnake

The rattlesnake, known as the "Terror of the Prairies", was one of the cowboy's most deadly enemies. Many hair-raising tales were told around the campfire about rattlesnakes.

Cut one sheet of 12" x 18" construction paper into six 18" strips. Connect strips, end to end, with brad fasteners. Draw a head on one end of snake and attach rattles made from a few pieces of macaroni strung on a wire to the other end. Paint or color the snake.

Broncos

A wiry, spirited horse — mustang, cayuse. Children make their own wild broncos. Use old socks for a bronco head. Stuff the sock with torn newspaper. Make ears from felt or paper and staple them to sides of horse's head. Use large brad fasteners for eyes. Attach horse head to a yardstick or other yard-length stick with tacks or tape. A leather or yarn string bridle may be tied around the horse's neck.

Sawhorses make good broncos. Children construct horse heads from scrap wood and add to sawhorses. Two boards are nailed together to make horse's neck and head. The neck is nailed to one end of the sawhorse. Add facial features with paint or markers. Yarn may be attached for a mane and tail. A leather string is tied around the neck of the horse for a bridle.

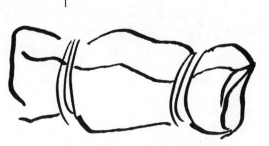

NATURE AND SCIENCE

Provide a display so children can explore.

- animal hides
- bale of hay
- branding irons
- cactus
- driftwood
- horns from cattle
- horseshoes
- rocks
- skeleton of head of cow
- snake skins
- tumbleweeds
- wildflowers

Blacksmith

The blacksmith makes and repairs horseshoes by hammering them on an anvil. The shoes are nailed to the hoof of the horse. A trip to a blacksmith, usually located in rural areas, informs children about the blacksmith's job.

Natural History Museum

Visit the natural history museum in your community to examine how different animals live. Contact the education department of the museum for more information and ask for a guide who can discuss animals, plants and the outdoor environment with young children.

If you live in an area similar to the dry regions in the west, observe the weather with the children and keep a record of your observations. Talk about how the dry weather effects

The knowledge and ideas the cowboy had about his natural surroundings were similar to, and perhaps borrowed from, the Plains tribes of the Native American. Cowboys valued their natural environment.

plants and animals. If you live where it rains a lot, talk about the differences between wet and dry weather and how plants and animals live in each climate.

Wildflower Walk

Children are always enthusiastic about taking a trip to a park, to a field or to the woods. Supply books about wildflowers, plants and insects in your community, and ditty bags and jars for collecting things from nature.

Wild Life

Books on armadillos, roadrunners, jackrabbits, longhorn cattle, buffalo, rattlesnakes and coyotes will encourage children to look for information about the characteristics of these animals.

LANGUAGE DEVELOPMENT

Vocabulary

Children are exposed to new words through materials and pictures about the cowboys in the room. As children role play the life of the cowboy and create things about cowboys, they will use some of these new words in their conversations with other children. Remember that each child may be interested in different words. Make a poster of some new words, placing the picture and word together. Some children will begin to write and read some words during their self-selected activities.

The following words are used in labeling pictures and objects in the room. This is a suggested list; other words may be added.

Print words on cards. Some children will copy the words. Others will read or match the words with pictures.

brand — a symbol identifying ownership. Each rancher has his own brand.

bridle — the headgear used to guide and control a horse when riding it. Two long strips of leather, called reins, run from the horse's mouth to the rider's hands.

bronco — a wild horse.

cattle — cows, bulls, calves.

chaps — leather leg-coverings worn by the cowboy to protect his legs.

chuck — food.

chuck wagon — the wagon in which the food and bedrolls are carried.

Many pictures, posters and books should be available to help the child become acquainted with the cowboy culture. These materials will stimulate language and use of new words. See the bibliography at the end of this section for names of books your local librarians will help you select from your public and school libraries.

corral — a fenced yard for cattle and horses.

dogie — a calf who has been abandoned by the cow.

drover — a man who drives cattle on the trail.

head — one animal.

lasso — a rope used to capture animals.

longhorn — a breed of cattle which has horns six feet long.

mane — the long hair on the horse's neck.

remuda — (ray MEW dah) — a collection of saddle horses.

rodeo — a contest when cowboys rope calves and ride wild broncos and bulls.

roundup — the gathering of cattle from the range.

rowel — a small wheel with sharp points fastened to the end of the spur.

rustler — a cattle thief.

slicker — a raincoat.

sombrero — a large Stetson hat with a high crown and wide brim.

spurs — metal prongs strapped to the cowboys' boots to help him control his horse.

steer — a bull which has been neutered.

tally book — a small pocket-sized record book used by rancher.

wrangler — a cowboy in charge of the horses.

Personal Stories

Children use some of the new words in their own stories. As a child dictates a story to an adult, the adult prints it on paper. The child usually watches how the adult prints the words. Children ask adults to "write" their stories when they have something to say rather than the adults imposing this activity on children. Not all children will be interested in dictating stories because of individual differences in rates of development.

Dramatization

Most often children make or select props needed for their roles in dramatizing stories. Some children need other children or adults to help them find suitable props. The adults will have a collection of items and materials in the room to satisfy the spontaneous requests of children.

Favorite cowboy stories for dramatization:
- COWBOYS: WHAT DO THEY DO
- THE CLUMSY COWBOY
- COWBOY ANDY

Storytime

Children's literature, both stories about real life and fiction, is an important way to learn about a culture. Stories provide authentic information about the culture. They are also powerful sources in introducing new words and giving children interesting ideas for talking, creating and dramatizing.

Storytime "happens" several times a day. A child brings a book, asks an adult to read it almost immediately; or he selects a book from the library, the book center. The book is often read to one child or to a small group of children. At times, all of the children are interested in hearing the same story.

Wild Tales

Some children will enjoy sitting around the campfire telling "wild tales" about their make believe adventures on the trail. This activity may be started by an adult who tells the first wild tale.

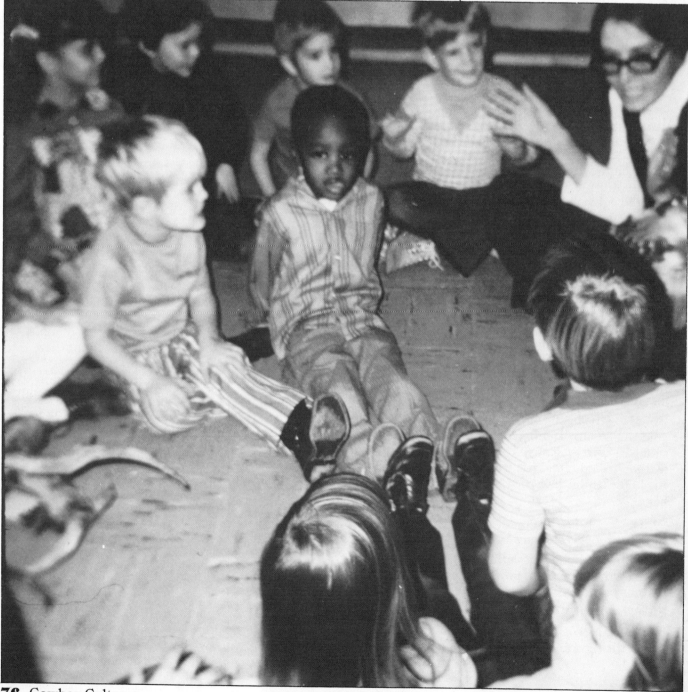

MUSIC AND DANCE

By Roger

Songs

Cowboy songs were created to quiet restless cattle or to move them to another place. They were also created to express feelings about the work and play of the cowboy. The musical quality of the song was not important, only the effect of the sound of the music.

Children sing and dance to cowboy lyrics. Examples are:

- THE BIG CORRAL
- BLUE TAIL FLY
- SKIP TO MY LOU

See bibliography for records.

Clog Dance

The Cowboy Clog dance is adapted from the clog dance in which the dancer wears wooden clog shoes to beat the time. The cowboy dances in his boots to the beat of the fiddle and to the clapping of the cowboys.

Musical Instruments

Guitars, harmonicas, fiddles and jew's harps accompany the singers and dancers.

GAMES AND MANIPULATIVES

Games

Outdoor activities for the cowboy included sitting around the campfire, telling tales and singing songs. They played games and had riding and roping contests. They also played many card games.

Craps

A game of dice. Children roll two dice. A first throw of 7 or 11 wins; a first throw of 2, 3, or 12 loses; any other first throw, to win, must be repeated until a 7 is thrown.

Cards

Children imitate cowboys playing cards.

Horseshoes

Hammer a stake into the ground. Children pitch horseshoes, one at a time, taking turns. The object of the game is to "ring" the stake with the horseshoe.

"Wrangler and the Rattler"

Children form a circle. Two children are chosen, one to be the "snake" and the other to be the "wrangler". Both are blindfolded and stand inside the circle. The "snake" shakes a covered tin can filled with stones. The "wrangler" holds a long stocking filled with paper to use as a club. The

The social life of the pioneer family included a mixture of recreation and work.

"wrangler" tries to find the "rattler" and hit the "rattler" with the stocking. If he hits the "rattler", the "rattler" chooses someone else to take his place.

Skipping Race

Skip, instead of hop, to turning line and back.

"One-Out"

Stones are placed at a finishing line. One less stone is placed than there are players. The players race from the starting line to the finishing line, each one trying to pick up a stone. The player who does not get one leaves the game and one stone is removed. The race continues until only one player remains.

"Husking Bee"

A husking bee was a favorite activity. When children prepare "corn-on-the-cob", they have a race to see which team can husk its corn first.

One Leg Race

Races were popular at gatherings and informal meetings. Each child holds one leg up and hops to a turning line, on the other foot, then hops back.

SPECIAL EVENTS

Western Art Museum

Take a trip to a Western Art Museum to see paintings and sculpture depicting the Old West.

Western Store

Take a trip to a western store to see the cowboy clothing people can buy today. Find out how boots and leather clothing are repaired.

Rodeo

Arrange for a tour to rodeo grounds when performances are not being held. This tour allows children to see "behind the scenes" of a rodeo. Plan an outing to a rodeo with parents.

Children enjoy staging their own rodeo—making and pinning contestant numbers on their backs, bucking out of a chute on their wild stick-broncos, and roping and tying up box-calves. Some children make flags and serve as judges.

Cookout

The End of the Trail activity for the study of the cowboy culture is a cook-out. Roundup Stew is prepared by the children for their parents.

Each child brings something for the stew—hamburger meat, canned tomatoes, green beans, corn, onions, carrots or potatoes.

Children peel potatoes, carrots and onions. They open cans and make meatballs. See cowboy recipes on previous pages.

Parents come to the evening roundup dressed in their cowboy clothes, and eat stew with the young cowboys at "The Learning Tree Ranch". Square dancing and singing to guitar music add to the festivities.

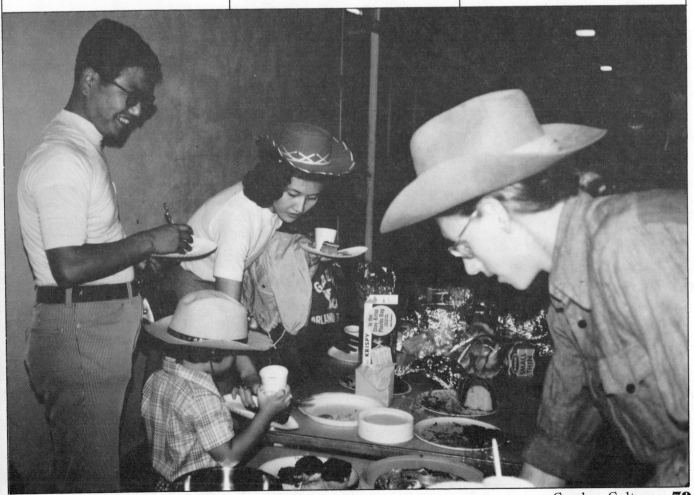

SELECTED BIBLIOGRAPHY

Cowboy Culture

Books for Children

Bailey, Bernadine. **Picture Book of Texas**. Whitman, 1967.
Illustrations by Kurt Wiese.

    About people who lived outdoors. Illustrations of familiar places in
Texas.

The Cowboys. Time-Life Books, 1973.

    Collection of recipes includes red bean pie and sourdough biscuits fit
for any child's appetite. Photographs of camps, range horses, a cowboy's
bunk and ranch houses engross young children.

Bronson, Wilfrid S. **Coyotes**. Harcourt, Brace and World, 1946.

    Natural science picture book describes habits of coyote with detailed
illustrations. Part of outdoor living experience.

Chandler, Edna. **Cowboy Andy**. Beginner Books, 1959. Illustrations
by E. Raymond Kintsler.

    Andy, a city boy, makes his first visit to a ranch.

Chenery, Janet. **Wolfie**. Harper & Row, 1969.

    Near to the heart of most young children is the study of insects and
bugs. Scenic book with many facts.

Glubok, Shirley. **The Art of the Old West**. Macmillan, 1971.

    Collection of paintings, sculpture and photographs of the Old West.
Young children are especially interested in this culture.

Greene, Carla. **Cowboys: What Do They Do?** Harper & Row,
1972.

    Excellent suggestions for activities for exploring outdoor living.
Branding, sleeping in a bedroll, roping cattle, riding bucking broncos and
singing around the campfire.

Hawkinson, John. **Let Me Take You On A Trail**. Whitman, 1972.

    To make a bow, climb a hill, swing on a vine, listen to the birds — is
experiencing the land. New ideas about things "to look for" on a nature
hike. Creative illustrations.

Honig, Donald. **In the Days of the Cowboy**. Random House,
1970.

    About authentic cowboy life. Dismisses any romantic images of the
cowboy. Authentic photos of the cowboy post Civil War period portray
cowboy life as difficult and unrewarding.

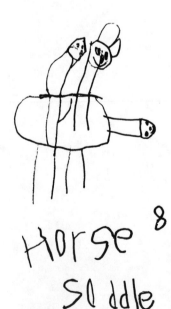

Horse
Saddle

Macdonald First Library. **Cowboys**. Macdonald Educational, 850 Seventh Avenue, New York, New York 10019.

Describes branding, living quarters, cattle drives, clothes and stampedes with illustrations and brief text. Gives credit to the vaquero for being the first models for American cowboy. "Native Americans fought bravely and fiercely to defend their living and hunting grounds."

McDowell, Bart. **The American Cowboy: The Life and Legend**. National Geographic Society, 1972.

Numerous colored photographs of all facets of cowboy life. Text for adults.

Malone, John. **Album of the American Cowboy**. Franklin Watts, 1971.

Working life of the cowboy. Includes large illustrations and authentic photographs of the activities pertaining to the roundup and trail drive.

Owens, William A. **Texas Folk Songs**. Texas Folk-Lore Society, SMU. Press, 1976.

Collection of songs from East Texas folk communities, Big Thicket area and the Mexican border. These areas are the best areas for an easy exchange of folk songs. Words and music with historical background material included. Be selective in using these songs.

Parish, Peggy. **Let's Be Early Settlers with Daniel Boone**. Harper & Row, 1967.

Children who wish to dress in the early pioneer dress will delight in this book crammed with ideas about how to make hats, hunting knives and shot pouches.

Peck, Leigh. **Pecos Bill and Lightning**. Houghton Mifflin, 1940.

Stories about Pecos Bill portray a strong, brave cowboy. Some of these "hero" tales can be told to young children. Omit the "wild Indian" images.

Reynolds, Robert. **The Cowboy: A Contemporary Photographic Study**. Graphic Arts Center Publishing Company, 2000 N.W. Wilson, Portland, Oregon 97209.

An experience in the daily life of the cowboy in modern day. "The pickup truck and trailer has revolutionized cowboyin'." Text with photographs gives a beautiful insight into the culture and romantic legend of ranching.

Ward, Don. **Cowboys and Cattle Country**. American Heritage, 1961.

The dirty, lonely life of the cowboy is described. Illustrations also point to the adventurous nature of the cowboy culture.

The children at the Learning Tree also enjoy these books. Look for them in your library.

Benet, Stephen V., **The Ballad of William Sycamore**
Bethell, Jean, **The Clumsy Cowboy**

Brown, Mark H. and W. R. Felton, **Before Barbed Wire**

Durham, Phillip and E. L. Jones, **The Adventures of the Negro Cowboy**

Floethe, Louise L., **The Cowboy on the Ranch**

Friskey, Margaret, **Indian Two Feet and Wolf Cubs**

Grant, Bruce, **The Cowboy Encyclopedia**

Harman, Fred, **The Great West in Paintings**

Landin, Les, **Cowboys Around the World**

Langmore, Bank and R. Tyler, **The Cowboy**

Monaghan, Jay, **The Book of the American West**

Munch, Theodore W. and M. V. DeVault, **Armadillo**

Munch, Theodore W. and M.V. DeVault, **The Roadrunner**

Smith, Erwin E., **Life on the Texas Range**

Books for Adults

Folsom, Franklin, **The Life and Legend of George McJunkin, Black Cowboy**, Elsevier-Nelson, 1973.

A biography of a Black cowboy who was well known for his skill with horses. He also discovered important archaelogical relics.

Hanes, Bailey C., **Bill Pickett, Bulldogger**. University of Oklahoma Press, 1977.

Biography of a Black cowboy.

Havighurst, Walter. **The First Book of Pioneers**. Franklin Watts, 1977.

Adult resource.

Rider, Rowland W., **Sixshooters and Sagebrush**, Brigham Young University Press, 1979.

Cowboy stories of the southwest.

Rollins, Philip A., **The Cowboy**. University of New Mexico Press, 1979.

Reprint of a 1936 book. History of life of cowboys on the old-time cattle range.

Rounds, Glen. **The Cowboy Trade**. Holiday House, 1972.

Informative book about the professional cowboy. Descriptions of cowboy's attire, pastime and work. Excellent resource for adults.

Savage, William W., **The Cowboy Hero**, University of Oklahoma Press, 1979.

Image of cowboy in American history and culture.

True, Henry A., **The Cowboy**, Newcomen Society in North America, 1980.

Contribution of cowboys to American culture.

White, John I., **Git Along, Little Dogies**, University of Illinois Press, 1975.

Songs and song makers of the American West.

Records and Films

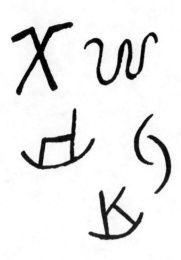

Cowboy Song Favorites, with Fay Willing. Allegro Dist: Record Corporation of America, Union City, New Jersey 07087. Record 1594

Music which lends itself to the outdoor-living atmosphere. "Blue Tail Fly", "Red River Valley" and "Tumbling Tumbleweeds" are included.

Do-Me-Ri Kids Hootenany, with Woody Guthrie and Pete Seeger. One record. Tom Glazier. Dist: Kapp Records, Division of M.C.A.. Inc., 100 Universal City Plaza, Universal City, California 91608. Record KL1360

This "small fry festival" includes selections from folk music. "Skip to My Lou", "Michael Row Your Boat Ashore", "Down in the Valley". Children dramatize, sing and dance to these songs.

Games and Rhythms, with Ella Jenkins. Folkways Records. Dist: Scholastic Records, 906 Sylvan Avenue, Englewood Cliffs, New Jersey 07632. Record FC7057

"Skip to My Lou" and "Blue Tail Fly" sung by Ella.

"The Big Corral", **Making Music Your Own**. Album 6 records. Silver Burdett Company. Dist: General Learning Corporation, 8301 Ambassador Road, Dallas, Texas 75247. Album 75180

This folk music involves children in song about horses. Book accompanies album.

Songs of Fox Hollow for Children of All Ages. Tom T. Hall. Phonogram, Inc., One IBM Plaza, Chicago, Illinois 60611.

A best seller for families. Includes "Sneaky Snake," "The Mysterious Fox of Fox Hollow," "How to Talk to a Little Baby Goat." One school made a huge stuffed sneaky snake!

"Cowboy: His Songs, Ballads and Brag Talk" Two 12" records. Folkway Records, address above. Record 5723.

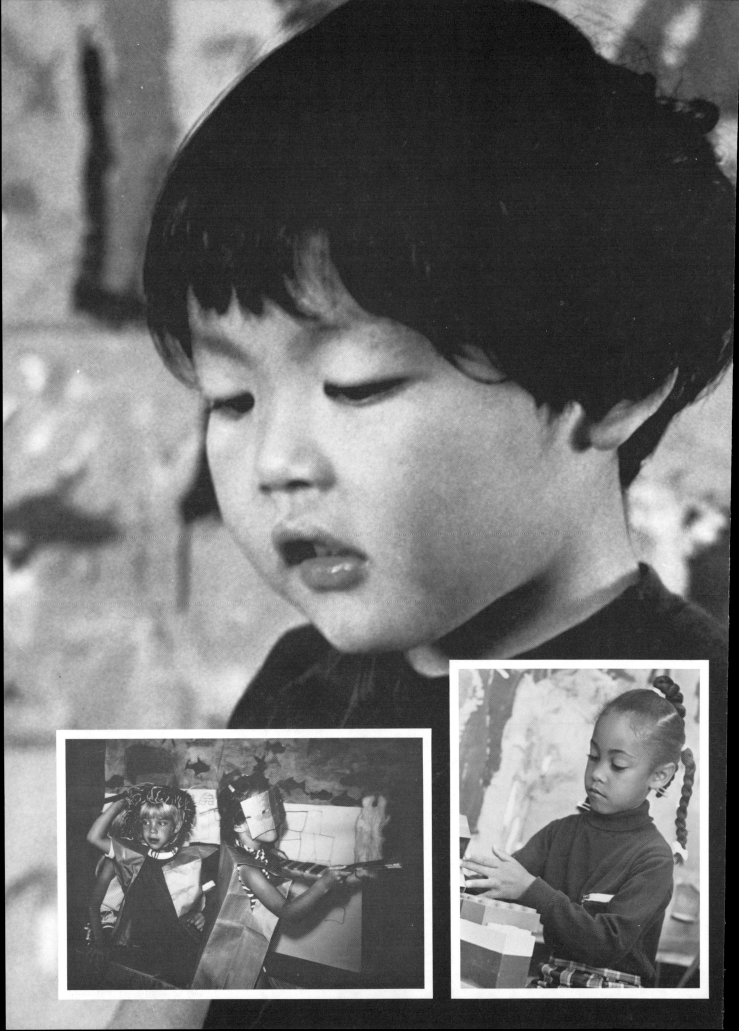

Eskimo Cultures

Searching for food across the cold lands of North America and building homes of driftwood and blocks of snow, the hardy people of the Arctic with their lifestyles and customs, capture the interest of young children.

This study describes the culture of the Eskimo. The five large Arctic groups are: Labradorians, Greenlanders, Central, Mackenzie and Alaskan Eskimos. The people have adapted their customs to the climate and weather of the cold Arctic country. Some of these customs have changed in modern times. To help you become culturally aware of the people in the north, both the traditional and the modern Eskimo cultures of the Arctic regions are described.

FAMILY LIVING

Homes

The shelter or home for an Eskimo family is the igloo. During winter days the home is a snow house, while in the summer the family lives in a tent similar to the round Indian tepee. Caribou hides are used for tents in the summer and for roofs of the snow houses in the winter. The snow house can be built in a hurry to provide shelter while on a hunting trip but it can also be used for a longer time. Some snow houses are round(ed) and some are

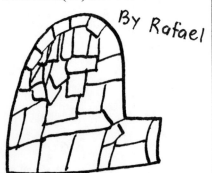

By Rafael

square. Where lumber is available underground homes are made. These homes are made of logs and sod. The sod is grass that is dug with the earth around the roots when the ground is not frozen.

Snow House

Snow igloos can be made by stretching 36" wide white butcher paper around sides of a card table. Children draw lines and squares with black markers to look like blocks of ice. A half-circle door can be cut in front.

Another way to make the snow igloo is to use a large cardboard box. Children paint the box with white paint using large brushes. Draw black lines and squares for blocks of ice.

Children can also use large wooden or cardboard blocks to build the igloo. Discuss the design of the snow house with children who are interested in designs.

Tents

The house that looks like a tent can be made by using an old bedspread or sheet stretched over a table or four chairs.

Children can sit in the tent, drink cold tea, chew on blubber and eat fish. At one time the Eskimo did not like hot food. Beef jerky can be substituted for blubber.

Subterranean House

Children can make subterranean or underground houses from boxes. Add furnishings for the home. Put up a wooden frame, supported by four poles, for drying clothes and boots. Eskimos also need lamps and dishes; and the children want dolls. Find large kettles for melting snow and for cooking stew.

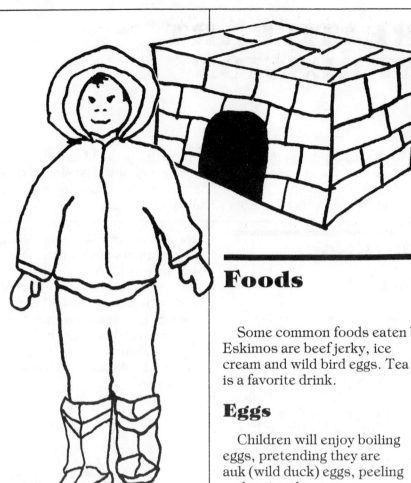

Household Articles

Furnish the "igloo" with a lamp, dishes, stove, tables, sleeping bags, and white and gray rabbit furs. Add Eskimo articles made by children. The directions are on the following pages.

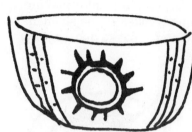

Foods

Some common foods eaten by Eskimos are beef jerky, ice cream and wild bird eggs. Tea is a favorite drink.

Eggs

Children will enjoy boiling eggs, pretending they are auk (wild duck) eggs, peeling and eating them.

Raw Fish

Bring cans of salmon, tuna and sardines. Children eat the fish on crackers, pretending they are raw fish.

Clothing

Boys and girls in some Eskimo cultures wear the same type clothing until about the age of eight. Then boys dress like men and girls dress like women.

Have the following clothing available for children. When they wear this clothing, they will feel and act like real Eskimos.
- parka
- boots
- mittens
- robes
- necklaces
- strips of fur to decorate clothing
- animal teeth to decorate trousers

Augutuk (Ice cream)

Augutuk (ice cream) is made with seal oil. Salmon berries are added. These berries are similar to strawberries.

2½ cups milk	1 teaspoon vanilla
3 tablespoons sugar	1 egg

Mix ingredients in an electric blender. Fill blender with cracked ice. Blend at high speed until thick. Top with a strawberry and pretend you are eating salmon berries.

CREATIVE ART EXPRESSION

Masks

As in other cultures, the Eskimo designs masks to honor the Spirits. They also create masks to amuse each other. Young children enjoy making comedy masks. The shaman and spirit masks may be jolly.

Masks to honor the Spirits

Elaborately decorated masks are used to enjoy life and to control the Spirits. Eskimos use masks in their dances. Hang animals, birds and body parts from the sides of the basic masks. Children draw and cut out these shapes and attach them to the mask with brass fasteners.

Feast Mask

Children decorate the outside of the bottom of 12" x 24" cardboard box as a mask. Hang the box from ceiling by attaching heavy string to box. Hang at a level so the child's face is behind the mask when he stands.

The creative handwork of the Eskimo artist is found in the decoration of the articles which are used every day. The skill of these woodworkers, and bone and ivory carvers is seen in masks, knives, boots and capes which have been made by hand.

Clothing

Parka

A fur jacket with a fur hood is an important piece of indoor and outdoor clothing for the Eskimo.

The parka is made by children. Cut arm holes in the narrow sides of a large grocery sack and a hole for the neck in the bottom of the sack. Cut the paper bag down the center of one wide side to the neck hole to make it look like a jacket.

To make the hood, cut out one large side from a lunch sack so that it fits the child's head like a hood. Glue cotton around cut edge for fur. Fasten strings to sides of sack and tie under chin.

Mukluks (boots)

Sealskin, walrus and reindeer provide fur for boots that have a grass and moss lining. These lightweight, warm and waterproof overshoes are worn over slippers made of birdskin.

Two lunch sacks can be decorated with Eskimo symbols and cotton glued around the top for fur. Put a sack on each foot and wrap strips of cloth or leather around the top of the sack to hold the sacks to the child's feet.

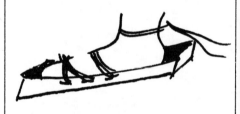

Snowshoes

Snowshoes enabled the Eskimo to walk over the snow. The North American Indians were the first cultures to use snowshoes when hunting and trapping. Eskimos make snowshoes of strings of animal hides stretched over a wood frame.

Children can make them by using the lids of shoe boxes. Place the lids upside down. Put the foot inside the center of the lid. Draw around the foot. Punch three holes on each side of the outline of the foot. Lace a strip of cloth or leather through these holes and over the foot. Wrap ends around the ankle and tie.

Capes

Waterproof capes are made from walrus intestines, gut strips and feathers. Make a cape from a piece of 36" x 36" cloth. Fasten ties at two top corners and tie around the neck. Add feathers and Eskimo designs.

Snow Goggles

Sunglasses are worn to protect the eyes from the glare of the sunlight from the snow. Eskimos make them from bone.

Children make the goggles by cutting two narrow slits in a 3" x 6" piece of cardboard. Attach strings to sides and tie around the head.

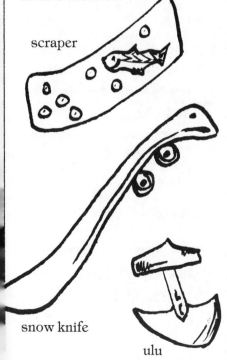

scraper

snow knife

ulu

Carving

The oldest Eskimo art was the carving of ivory from tusks of the walrus. Today Eskimo artists make carvings from a dark stone called soapstone. The Eskimo selects a piece of ivory or soapstone and looks at it, talks to it and sings to it for many days. This is a special event in his life. Later he carves it into a beautiful work of art— an animal, a spear or an Eskimo.

Children may imitate the Eskimo and scrape on a bar of dark-colored soap until a shape is carved—a shape that is "waiting inside the tusk".

Household Articles

Scraper

Eskimos used a scraper to clean animal hides. We believe that the Eskimo, when designing tools, decorated them and made them beautiful. The beautiful tools were used in everyday life.

The ivory scraper, decorated with the very old Eskimo dot and circle design, is recreated by the children. The snow knife is an example of this design.

Snow Knives

The Eskimo can build a snow house in an hour. They have learned to use the ice and snow around them. A snow knife is made of ivory from the walrus and is used for cutting snow into blocks.

Some children draw and cut the shape of a knife on a 3" x 12" piece of cardboard. They wrap the handle with a strip of cloth.

Ulu (OO loo)

The ulu, the woman's knife, is used to cut the seal and to peel the skin from the blubber.

This thin skin is used as wrapping paper by the Eskimo.

Children chew leather strips to soften them the same way the Eskimo woman prepares the hides. Children make an ulu by cutting a half-moon from an 8" x 8" piece of cardboard.

Hunting

The cold country and long winters of the Eskimo challenges the imagination of these people. They have developed special skills to cope with their surroundings. Because of the climate, few trees grow in most areas. Therefore, hunting equipment is made from parts of animals. Animals also supply food, clothing and ivory.

Snow House

The Eskimos name all houses igloos, whether they are made of driftwood, stone or ice. The most creative invention of the Eskimo is the snowhouse, a temporary home for the nomads, made of blocks of snow.

The snow house can be made as part of a small Eskimo village. To make snow, children mix three cups of ivory flakes with one cup of water. Whip with an electric beater until stiff. Children spread this soap mixture on the surface of a large board which is used as a foundation. Snow houses can be added by using single sections of an egg carton covered with "snow". Small Arctic animals may be drawn by the children and placed in the snow. Add mirrors for lakes.

Harpoon

The harpoon is a special spear with a line attached. The

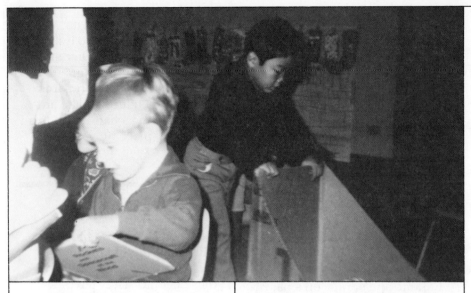

hunter holds onto the thong or leather strip that is tied to the harpoon and throws the harpoon at the animal.

Tape a cardboard spear hook to a 36" stick. Tie a piece of yarn or a leather strip to the other end of the stick for the thong. This harpoon can be thrown at a target drawn in the shape of a seal or a whale.

Kayak

The Eskimo, in search of food, moves with the seasons, sometimes on water and sometimes on land.

The kayak is a canoe made from driftwood and sealskin. It holds only one man.

Umiak (OO-me-ak)

The umiak is the woman's boat and it is used for the family. It is wider and longer than the man's canoe so more people can ride in it.

Children can make the kayak or umiak out of a large cardboard box. Cut one wide side open. Close all the other sides of the box. Children paint the canoe and decorate it with Eskimo designs.

Komatik

The Eskimo name for sled is Komatik. Sleds are made of driftwood, leather strips, bone antlers and ivory. These sleds are drawn by a team of huskies or dogs.

Children can make a sled. Place two 2" x 24" pieces of wood parallel to each other, one foot apart. Nail six 2" x 12" strips of cardboard to these runners. Add a hitch by nailing one 36" leather strip to one end of each runner.

Another type of Eskimo sled can be made from a large cardboard box. Cut one end of the box open. This end is the front of the sled. Cut 2 sides of the box diagonally from the top to the bottom, starting at the back. Cut the top triangle off of each side.

Nets

Greenland Eskimos designed a net to catch small birds, auks, which come to the northern part of the island on the exact day the last snow melts in the spring. A catch of eight auks is a good meal for one adult.

To make nets, children shape a circle out of a wire coat hanger which has been straightened by unwinding the wire. Starting at one corner of a 24" square of net, weave the wire hanger through the edges of the four sides, forming a circle out of half of the wire. Leave the other half of the wire for the handle. Close the circle by bending the end of the wire. Children use these nets outdoors. Children dramatize catching auks. These nets can also be used for catching butterflies and insects.

Ball

A lightweight ball made of animal skin stuffed with moss is used to play catch-ball.

These balls are similar to the American "sockie" or rag ball and can be made from cloth rags substituted for skin. If moss is not available for the center of the ball, a stone or piece of clay is suitable. Children are encouraged to select one the size of a large marble. Three-fourths inch strips are torn from a piece of bed sheet or cloth. These cloth pieces are tied together to make one long strip. A long strip of cloth is required to make a rag ball. Some children rip the cloth and others cut it with scissors. Some children, with adult help, can wrap the strip around the marble until the size meets the child's approval. To make the ball last longer, sew the raw edges of the strips.

Mural

Children paint snow pictures with white paint on a large piece of paper. They will add other colors as they add to the winter scene to include animals, homes and people.

Aurora Borealis

Children apply colored chalk to dark paper to give the effect of northern lights.

NATURE AND SCIENCE

Displays

Display natural materials. These items are used for sensory experiences as well as for informing children about types of materials that are used by Eskimos to make clothing, household articles and tents.

- bones, horns, tusks and skin
- animal furs — fox, rabbit, wolf and bear
- stones, clay, driftwood and moss

Food

Eskimos drink melted ice. All drinking water in the Arctic is melted snow or ice. The older the ice, the less salt it contains and the better it tastes.

ESKIMOS KNEW is an excellent book for scientific experiments.

Snow Ice Cream

If snow is available, make snow ice cream.

2 quarts snow
½ cup milk

1 teaspoon vanilla
¼ cup sugar

Combine ingredients in a bowl and mix. Add more snow if it is more slushy than desired.

Ice cream can also be prepared in a freezer according to directions for the freezer.

Children observe the salt as it melts the chunks of ice. Children ask many scientific questions about this experience.

A container of ice gives children a chance to observe how ice melts. They drink the water and compare the taste of melted ice with water from the faucet. Compare the taste of salty and plain water.

Blubber

Blubber is fuel that comes from seals, walruses and whales. It is also one of the most important foods for Eskimos. Children can chew beef jerky or dried beef as a substitute for blubber.

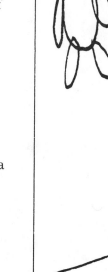

SEAL

Whale

LANGUAGE DEVELOPMENT

Vocabulary

The following words are used in labeling pictures and objects in the room.

Eskimo (ESS kih moh) — an Indian word meaning "eaters of raw flesh".

shaman (SHAH mun) — medicine man who wears special masks to keep evil spirits from doing any harm.

parka — coat with a hood of cotton or skin. Mothers carry babies in hoods and a belt is tied around the waist to hold hood in place.

igloo — house.

mukluks (MUK luks) — sealskin boots.

auks — small birds.

tundra — level land of frozen ground.

kayak (KA yak) — boat for one man.

umiak (OO mi ak) — family boat with oars and a sail, made of intestines from the seal which are sewn together.

husky — dogs used to pull sleds.

ulu (OO loo) — woman's knife used for preparing animals for food and clothing.

harpoon — spear with a line attached.

caribou — Arctic deer which supplies food, tools and toys.

cat's cradle — string game played by Eskimos.

narwhal — Arctic mammal with 9-foot tooth.

Language varies in the five Arctic regions. However, all Eskimos understand each other. Eskimoan is the basic language and it is a very complicated one.

Aurora Borealis (aw ROH ruh BOH re AY lis) — northern lights that shine when streams of tiny electrical particles from the sun hit the outer air around the earth.

Anaghalook — name for girl.

Silook — name for boy.

Yatelin — name for boy.

Joshua

ESKimo
harpoon

By Kumiko

JOHN

Phillip

Illustrations

Some children make an Eskimo booklet. Cut paper for the pages in the shape of an igloo. Fasten pages together. Children draw Eskimo symbols and designs in their books or print their favorite Eskimo words. Adults print the stories dictated by the children.

Favorite stories for dramatization:

- LOKOSHI LEARNS TO HUNT SEALS
- A PUPPY NAMED GHI
- INATUK'S FRIEND
- OOTAH'S LUCKY DAY

The Arctic region is the home of animals who adapt to cold weather and to isolated lands. Some animals migrate to the Arctic land for the summer. Most of the children want to paint or draw whales and norwhals because they have unusual characteristics.

Whales are some of the largest animals which have ever lived on this earth. They blow water as they come to the top of the water for air. The norwhal has a tooth projecting nine feet from the front of its jaw. The white whale changes color from dark gray to yellow. Young children are very interested in discussing and illustrating the special features of snow owls, tundra hares, snow geese and polar bears.

Books with pictures of animals are:

- DWELLERS OF THE TUNDRA: LIFE IN AN ALASKAN ESKIMO VILLAGE
- ALASKA
- POLAR DESERTS

MUSIC
AND DANCE

By Laura

When Eskimo families gather to spend the evening eating and drinking, entertainment is a part of the festivities. Sometimes one Eskimo is considered to be the best singer and he is expected to act as a song leader. Children change words and dance to the rhythms of the music. The singer ends the song with a shriek and everyone laughs.

Children come together and take turns entertaining each other with songs, dances and stories. They drink the hot tea they have brewed and eat fish, such as salmon or sardines. (See bibliography for recording.)

GAMES AND MANIPULATIVES

The recreation of the Eskimo depends upon the season of the year.

Outdoor Games

In the summer, when hunters are able to hunt for long hours, the Eskimos play games outdoors.

Ball Games

Eskimos play several kinds of ball games. They hit the ball with a hand in the direction of their opponent. The first person to get the ball kicks it and races across the field as in kick ball.

Small balls are used for "catch ball". These games are played with lightweight balls made of skin and stuffed with moss. Instructions for making balls are in this chapter.

Trading

Eskimo life includes the days spent trading with neighbors at the Post.

Children imitate the custom of trading by carrying fur and other articles they have made in a bag. They offer the articles to each other for trade.

Fishing

Children draw fish of different sizes and cut them out. Fasten a paper clip to the head of each fish and put it into a container. Make a fish line by tying a string to a small round magnet with a hole in the middle. Use the fishing line to "fish" for salmon.

Additional Outdoor Eskimo Games:

- relay races
- jump rope
- wrestling

Indoor Games

Games are played with people sitting on the floor close to each other in a crowded room.

Storytelling

Telling humorous stories and making funny faces is a popular entertainment for Eskimos. The object of these activities is to make people giggle or laugh. The first person to laugh is the next one to make a face.

Stories about brave acts are favorites with Eskimos. See the book, THE ESKIMO, ARCTIC HUNTERS AND TRAPPERS, for some stories.

Cat's Cradle

Cat's cradle is a string game. Children play it with a long string. A child twists the string around the fingers of both hands to make a design.

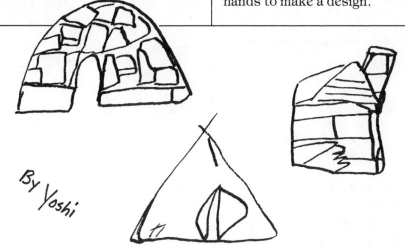

By Yoshi

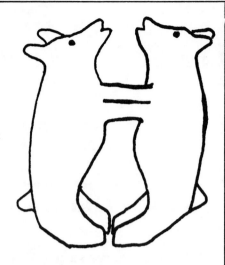

Carving

When men sit in the igloo at night, they carve toys, tools and ornaments from wood, stone and ivory.

Spinning a Top

Carved tops of wood, bone, stone or clay are spun by Eskimo children on a hard piece of walrus hide. Adults can demonstrate how to spin a top.

Bow Drill

Display the bow drill Eskimos used for starting a fire, for carving and drilling ivory. Children like to examine it and try it out on a piece of wood.

"Bones"

Each Eskimo child has a set of carved bones in the shape of animals. The "bones" are tossed into the air. When they land, the player who has the most animals standing or facing her, is the winner.

Children can substitute plastic animals to imitate this game.

Sewing

The Eskimo places value on expert sewing. The wife uses caribou sinews for thread. Sinews make a very strong thread.

Some children sew articles using a needle, thread and a cloth. Use large crewel needles with blunt ends.

Manipulatives

• View Master with reels of Eskimos.
• Blocks for sorting, stacking and building igloos.

SPECIAL EVENTS

The Inviting-In Feast

The Inviting-In Feast is the first annual ceremony in Alaska. This celebration is held in honor of the animals.

After some children have made masks they may come together to dance and to chant. Hang the masks children have made from the ceiling. The young creators stand behind them. The feast mask is described in this chapter. The masks can be part of the Inviting-In Feast.

North Star Day

North Star Day is an event at Shishmaref, Alaska. A ship, filled with canned milk, butter, apple juice, oatmeal cookies, syrup and other special foods for the Eskimos of this isolated village, makes its annual port of call or visit to the village.

Young children dramatize North Star Day. Children can unload the ship's supply of "fruit juice". The celebration can include dancing and dining on a treat of fruit juice or milk with oatmeal cookies.

Other Activities

•Visit an exhibit of Eskimo art at a museum in your community.
•View special Eskimo exhibits in your community.

SELECTED BIBLIOGRAPHY

Eskimo Cultures

Books for Children

Brewster, Benjamin. **The First Book of Eskimos**. Franklin Watts, 1952.

    Read to young children. Told from personal view of a family. Illustrations are descriptive.

Claiborne, Robert. **The First Americans**. Time-Life Books, 1973.

    Gives insight into the history and rich cultural background of the Eskimos, Northwest Indians, Southwest Indians and the Mound Builders. Photographs and drawings illustrate text.

Clymer, Theodore. **The Travels of Atunga**. Little, Brown, 1973.

    Example of language and lifestyle of Eskimo culture. Atunga seeks help from Tungarsug and Sedna, "gods that the Eskimo fears."

Field, Edward, ed. **Eskimo Songs and Stories**. Delacorte, 1973.

    A collection of literature and print showing the soul of the rugged life of "the people of the seal."

Ginsburg, Mirra, ed. **The Proud Maiden, Tungah, and the Sun**. Macmillan, 1974.

    Adventure of a woman as she flees from an evil spirit of the Tundra.

Herbert, Wally. **Polar Deserts**. Watts, 1971.

    Text for adults and full-page color photographs of dog teams, Eskimo families and animals for children and adults.

Hunt, Karis, and B.W. Carlson. "Eskimo Masks of Alaska", **Masks and Mask Makers**. Abingdon Press, 1961, 24-26.

    Brief text describes a shaman and his many duties. Children can make masks, dance, play tambourines and call to the spirit in a secret language.

Metayer, Maurice, ed. **Tales from the Igloo**. Hurtig, 1972.

    The Eskimo relied on verbal communication to pass on his history and traditions. Select stories carefully. Information about changes in the culture today.

Newell, Edythe W. **The Rescue of the Sun and Other Tales of the Far North**. Whitman, 1970.

    Introduction acquaints readers with the Eskimo cultures and conditions surrounding the folktales.

Rasmussen, Knud. **Beyond the High Hills: A Book of Eskimo Poems**. Philomel Books, 1961.

Young children enjoy the large photographs of animals, homes, clothing, snowhouse. Exceptional resource.

Parish, Peggy. **Ootah's Lucky Day**. Harper & Row, 1970.

This "I can Read" book is an exciting tale of an Eskimo boy on a walrus hunt who is confronted by a bear. Ootah outwits the bear and takes home a walrus, qualifying himself as a hunter. Motivates dramatization.

Pine, Tillie S. **The Eskimos Knew**. McGraw-Hill, 1962. Illustrations by Ezra J. Keats.

Engages children in scientific experiments and crafts. Shows Eskimos as conservationists.

Scott, Ann H. **On Mothers' Lap**. McGraw-Hill, 1972.

Story about sharing. Offers a realistic view of life in one Alaska community.

Stefanssen, Evelyn. **Here is Alaska**. Scribner's Sons, 1959.

Text for older children but can be adapted for younger children. Full-page photographs of seals, caches, Eskimos and umiaks.

The children at the Learning Tree also enjoy these books. Look for them in your library.

Berrill, Jacquelyn, **Wonders of the Arctic**
Butler, Evelyn and G.A. Dale, **Alaska: The Land and the People**
Hermanns, Ralph, **Children of the North Pole**
Hopkins, Marjorie, **The Three Visitors**
Lewis, Richard, **I Breathe a New Song: Poems of the Eskimo**
Mayberry, Genevieve, **Eskimo of the Little Diomede**
Keating, Bern, **Alaska**
Machetanz, Sara, **A Puppy Named Gih**
Stull, Edith, **The First Book of Alaska**
Tompkins, Stuart R., **Life in America, Alaska**
Vevers, Gwynne, **Animals of the Arctic**

Books for Adults

Bleeker, Sonia. **The Eskimo: Arctic Hunters and Trappers** Morrow, 1959.

Sections on customs and hunting. Helps understanding of scarcity of game.

Breltweld, Jim. **Getting to Know Alaska**. Coward-McCann, 1958.

Text for adults and older children. Illustrations of ivory carvings, kayak lessons, sledge riding and the celebration of "Nullikulltick".

Coles, Robert, **The Last and First Eskimos**. New York Graphic Society, 1978.

One of many books on cultures by a psychiatrist who truly understands "cultures." Text is from personal interviews. Many excellent black and white photographs of life of Eskimo today.

By Antonio

by Kiersten

Collins, Henry B. and others, **The Far North**. Indiana University Press and the National Gallery of Art, 1977.

Pictures show 2000 years of American Eskimo and Indian art from the far north, Alaska. Photographs were taken in many museum collections from all over the world. Among the topics are clothing, jewelry, masks and fishing.

Comins, Jeremy, **Eskimo Crafts and Their Cultural Backgrounds**. Lothrop, 1975.

The Eskimos developed skill in carving tools and weapons from stone, ivory and driftwood for hunting and fishing. Designs are simple without much detail. Children will adapt the ideas for their artistic needs.

Eber, Dorothy. **Pitseolak: Pictures Out of My Life**. University of Washington Press, 1971.

A bilingual autobiography (English-Eskimo) about the life of a woman Eskimo artist. Many black and white pictures. Covers the time from early 1900's to 1970. Dispels many myths about the Eskimos.

Hall, Edwin S. **The Eskimo Storyteller**. University of Tennessee Press, 1975.

Folktales from Noatak, Alaska.

Jenness, Aylette. **Dwellers of the Tundra: Life In An Alaskan Eskimo Village**. Macmillan, 1970.

Text for adult is excellent and informative. Exceptional and authentic photographs of homes and people in black and white.

Judge, Joseph. "Alaska: Rising Northern Star", **National Geographic**. 147, (June, 1975), 731-791.

Describes event at Shishmaref when ship makes its annual port of call.

Mary-Rousselier, Guy. "I Live With the Eskimos," **National Geographic**, 139, (February, 1971), 188-217.

Article about Canadian Eskimo. Includes photographs of hunting narwhals, landscapes and families.

Pitseolak, Peter and D. Eber. **People From Our Side**, Indiana University Press, 1977.

Eskimo life story in words, with black and white photographs. Illustrations of Eskimo writing. From a story told by a 71 year old Eskimo about life on Baffin Island. Very different from our stereotypes of the Eskimos.

Ray, Dorothy J., **Eskimo Art**, University of Washington Press, 1977.

Traditional and innovative art from northern Alaska.

Senungetuk, Joseph E., **Give or Take a Century: An Eskimo Chronicle**, Indian Historian Press, 1971.

Written by an Eskimo for his people, to help them learn their own history and culture. Clear descriptions and illustrations of their life.

Wells, James K., **Ipani Eskimos**, 1974, Alaska Methodist University Press, Anchorage, Alaska 99504.

Describes the outdoor activities of the Eskimos for each month of the year. Realistic pictures of Eskimo life today. Excellent information! Other books by same publisher are **People of Kauwerak** by William A. Oquilluk and Dolores Kawagley; **Yupik Stories** and **Eskimo Legends** by Lela K. Oman.

Magazines

Alaska Geographic
Quarterly
Alaska Geographic Society, P.O. Box 4-EEE, Anchorage, AL 99509.

Each issue is based on a theme, developed with an essay and color photographs. Authentic information.

Alaska Journal
Quarterly
Alaska Georgraphic Society, address above.

Devoted to the historical and cultural heritage of Alaska and northern Canada. Emphasis is on the past, with news about some contemporary artists and their art.

Records and Films

The Eskimos of Hudson Bay and Alaska. Folkways Records and Service Corporation. Dist: Folkways Scholastic Records, 906 Sylvan Avenue, Englewood Cliffs, New Jersey 07632.
Record FE4444.

Authentic Eskimo songs for playing games, dancing and hunting. Recorded on Hudson Bay by Laura Boulton and the Eskimos of that area.

The White Dawn. Paramount. Dist: American Film Company. 110 minutes.

Documentary of Northern Canadian Eskimo. Culture has been preserved and most of it is traditional and primitive. The film provides viewer an insight into daily activities of the nomadic group.

Mexican Cultures

Mexican American
Mexican Heritage

Mexican Americans were among the first cultures to settle in southwestern United States. They brought with them customs and traditions from the varied cultures in the six main regions of Mexico. At the same time, they adapted the Mexican customs and traditions to their new environment and began some customs of their own. Today, some Mexican Americans have been natives in America for several generations. Some Mexicans came to America a long time ago while other Mexicans have been in this country only a short time.

Become acquainted with the Mexican Americans and people from other Hispanic cultures in your community. Find out which traditional customs are observed by these families.

Many Americans from Mexican and Hispanic cultures are bilingual. They speak the Spanish language in their homes and to their Spanish speaking friends. They also speak English when they live and work in the community.

The goal of becoming aware of the Mexican and Mexican American cultures is to expose children to these cultures, to help them appreciate the rich Mexican heritage, and to understand the great variations within the Mexican and Mexican American cultures.

FAMILY LIVING

Clothing

Mexican Americans and city dwellers in Mexico wear clothing similar to the styles worn in North America and Europe. Because the clothes worn by the rural people in Mexico are different and express the traditional culture of Mexico, teachers provide these traditional costumes for dramatizing Mexican roles.

Provide Mexican clothing and furnishings for children. These are available at Mexican import shops, or they might be borrowed from Mexican American parents or friends in the community, who have traveled in Mexico.

Some clothing children especially enjoy wearing is:

huraches — leather sandals.

vestidas — vests made from woven fabric that is something like a blanket.

rebozos — colorful shawls worn by Mexican women.

mantilla — a large lace head scarf worn by Mexican women.

sarape — a colorful blanket worn over the shoulder by Mexican men.

skirts — long, full skirts worn by villagers and as costumes.

cotton shirts and trousers — informal dress for Mexican men.

sombreros — wide-brimmed Mexican hats.

Children get a glimpse of the rural and urban Mexican life and of some of the Mexican American families. Lifestyles vary according to climate and money. Patios and houses of adobe bricks, rebozos and huraches, tamales and atole, parades and bullfights, attract young children.

Furnishings

Other furnishings are:

- Mexican dolls
- straw baskets
- bowls and vases made of pottery
- small wooden chairs from Mexico
- tortilla press for real or play-dough tortillas
- pinatas — an item used for a game during fiestas
- Mexican jewelry

Families Celebrate

Fiesta Party

Different communities celebrate different fiestas or holidays. Find out which holidays are celebrated by the Mexican Americans and Mexicans in your community. The way holidays are celebrated in the United States by Mexican Americans are similar in many ways to the way Mexicans celebrate fiestas. They can

include wearing of the special holiday costumes, games, dances, pinatas and bullfights. Yet, the Mexican Americans in each community may make some changes, adding some activities and omitting others. They also celebrate the American holidays.

After children have role-played Mexican family life, they plan a fiesta. They invite their families to the fiesta.

Foods and Cooking Experiences

Frijoles (Beans)

Print directions on a poster in English and Spanish so the children are exposed to the idea that words can be read and directions followed.

Wash (Lava):
1 pound dried pinto beans

Water (Aqua):
Add 2 quarts water
small piece salt pork
salt to taste

Cook (Cocina):
Beans until tender—about 2½ hours

Eat (Come):
Serve with tortillas

Tortillas (Bread)

Tortilla is the basic bread in Mexico. It is round and thin, and made of corn flour.

Masa harina, a fine corn flour, is available in many grocery stores.

Children can make tortillas with the tortilla press or they can shape them with their hands.

Mix (Mezclar):
2 cups masa
1 cup water
Make small balls.

Press (Prensar):
Press ball flat until it is round and then…

Cook (Cocina):
Heat a large ungreased skillet or griddle and drop tortillas one at a time onto the skillet. Brown on one side, then turn and brown on the other side.

Eat (Come):
Serve with butter or with beans.

Children take turns using the press and frying their own tortillas.

Atole

Make atole, a soupy cornmeal mush, eaten in Mexican homes. Instant grits made into a thin soup is similar to atole. Follow the recipe on the box.

Chile

4 pounds ground beef
2 teaspoons chopped garlic
2 tablespoons shortening
4 teaspoons ground cominos
½ cup chili powder
4 tablespoons flour
2 tablespoons salt
2 teaspoons pepper
6 cups water

Lightly brown ground beef and garlic in hot fat, stirring with fork to crumble beef. Cover and cook on low heat for 15 minutes. Combine cominos, chili powder, flour, salt and pepper; add to cooked meat and stir well. Add water and cook slowly for 1 hour. Serves 12.

Enchiladas

48 tortillas
4 tablespoons shortening
4 pounds natural grated cheese
6 onions, chopped

Dip tortillas in heated oil. Place 1 tablespoon of cheese and 1 teaspoon of onion in the center of each tortilla. Roll tortilla and place in large baking dish, seam-side down. Cover with chili. Top with cheese and onions. Bake at 350 degrees for 15 to 20 minutes until cheese melts. Serves 24.

Tacos

This recipe came from a Mexican American mother who made them with the children at school.

Fry (Frito):
Brown 1 pound ground meat in a frying pan

Mix (Mezclar):
1 package taco seasoning after meat is browned

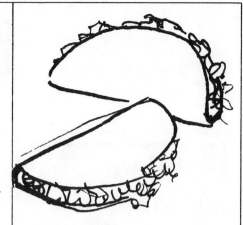

Mix and fill:
Taco shells with 2 tablespoons of the meat mixture

Prepared taco shells may be purchased or tortillas can be made, cooked and folded in half. Top with grated cheese, chopped lettuce and diced tomatoes.

Pan dulce
A sweet bread for supper by many villagers

Mix (Mezclar):
1 box of hot roll mix, prepare according to directions on package

Knead (Amasar):
Give each child enough dough for one roll. Each child kneads his dough and forms a ball.

Bake (Hornear):
As directed on package

Glaze top of roll (Vidriar):
With 2 cups powdered sugar
3 tablespoons milk
1 teaspoon vanilla

Mexican Hot Chocolate

Mix in a cup:

1 teaspoon cocoa
3 teaspoons sugar
1/3 cup powdered milk
½ teaspoon cinnamon

Fill cup with hot water, stir Top with 1 tablespoon whipped cream.

CREATIVE ART EXPRESSION

Clothing

Traditional costumes are purchased, but the following costumes can be made by the children.

The traditional dress of men living in Mexican villages was bright-colored serapes or blankets. The men wore them during cold and rainy weather.

Sarapes (Blankets)

Children make sarapes by using a 12" x 36" piece of unbleached cotton fabric. The

Mexico is a country known for its artists. Mexicans living in the villages make many of the items they use by hand. Mexicans have passed on a love and respect for handcrafts from generation to generation.

book **Pancho** has illustrations of beautifully designed sarapes or wraps. Children use felt tip markers or crayons to decorate sarape with their own designs.

Poncho

Ponchos are worn by men, women and children in Mexico

and in the southwest as a wrap. They are blankets with a slit in the middle for the head.

Provide 18" x 36" pieces of old sheets or unbleached cotton fabric. Fold in half and cut a slit in the middle large enough to go over a child's head. Children fringe the bottom of the poncho. They decorate the poncho with their own designs using felt-tip markers or crayons.

Rebozo (Shawl)

Rebozos are colorful shawls worn by Mexican women. They are used by mothers for carrying their babies. Babies are wrapped inside the rebozo close to the body of the mother.

Children can make rebozos using the same method as for making the sarapes.

Poblana (Skirt)

This costume for women is usually worn in the jarabe tapatico, the "Mexican Hat Dance". The poblana is a red and green full skirt decorated with beads and sequins.

Children can make the poblana by applying glitter to a crepe paper skirt or to a ready-made skirt. They paint designs on the skirt with glue and then sprinkle glitter over the glue. Be sure to put newspapers under the skirt when adding the glitter. Save the unused glitter for future activities.

Charro Suit

The charro suit is worn by Mexican men for holiday celebrations. This suit includes a bolero, which is a short jacket, trousers, shirt and a flowing red bow for a tie.

To make an inexpensive bolero, use plastic wall covering fabric. Any type of fabric or heavy paper can be used. An 18" x 24" piece of fabric makes one bolero. Adults cut out three pieces to make a jacket. Children punch holes on each side of the jacket and lace the sides with yarn or fasten the sides with large brad fasteners. Make the bow tie of red crepe paper or fabric.

Sashes

Wide colorful handwoven sashes are worn by Mexican women and men.

Children draw animals, plants or other designs on a 3" x 36" piece of unbleached cotton fabric or old sheet. Children tie this sash around their waist or head.

Jewelry

Mexicans living in the village make many of the items they use, such as jewelry, by hand. Mexico is known for its beautiful silver handcrafted jewelry. A display of jewelry items and pictures will help the children appreciate the artistry and skill of the Mexican craftsmen. Mexican silver rings, pins, necklaces and bracelets should be available for children to wear and to examine.

Necklaces and Bracelets

Children can make imitations of this jewelry in several ways. Necklaces and bracelets can be made by stringing bottle caps and metal disks on yarn or colored pipe cleaners. Children punch holes in the caps and the disks with a hammer and nail. The hammer and nail activity is one children really enjoy.

Semi-precious stones and materials are used by Mexicans to make pieces of jewelry. The stones are polished and strung to make beads.

Clay Beads

Soda-Cornstarch Clay

Mix: 1 cup cornstarch
2 cups soda
Add: 1¼ cups cold water and mix

Cook and stir over medium heat about four minutes to the consistency of mashed potatoes. Cover with damp cloth and cool. Knead just like kneading yeast dough. Several drops of food coloring may be added to make different colors of beads.

Children form small marble-sized balls out of clay. Put holes in the center of each ball with a toothpick. Bake for 1 hour at 200 degrees. If oven is not available, clay beads will dry in about 24 hours in the sun. String the dried beads on colored pipe cleaners to make bracelets and necklaces. Connect several pipe cleaners for longer necklaces.

Fiesta Decorations

The fiesta is the main recreation for most Mexicans and many Mexican Americans participate.

After children are costumed and bejeweled, they decorate the room for a village fiesta. Children make decorations such as paper flowers, pinatas and Mexican flags. Authors of books who describe fiestas suggest many other decorations. Such books are
- LET'S TRAVEL IN MEXICO
- PIZORRO
- THE TOY TRUMPET.

Tissue Paper Flowers

Paper flowers from Mexico can be bought in import shops but children can also make them.

To make one flower, cut four 6" x 10" pieces of bright-colored tissue paper. Lay the four pieces on top of each other. Gather tissue paper together in the center for bow-tie effect. Wrap a colored pipe cleaner around the center. Then pull each layer apart to make the flower. These paper flowers are beautiful in the room and in the hair of young senoritas!

Pinata

During the **Posada** Season from December 16th to 24th, many pinata parties are held. Goodies are placed in a big clay jar. The jar is covered with paper mache or layers of crepe paper and decorated with colorful designs. Mexicans use peanuts, sugar cane, candy and toys to fill the pinata. The pinata game involves blindfolding the children, taking turns trying to break the pinata with a stick and scrambling for the goodies.

To make a pinata, children tape crepe paper streamers of various lengths around the sides and on the bottom of a large grocery bag. Tape the streamers so that they hang down around the bag and cover it. Fill the bag with goodies like candy, nuts, gum and trinkets. Tape the open end of the pinata shut. Tie a strong string to the sides of the pinata and hang it from the ceiling. A stick for hitting the pinata can be decorated with crepe paper streamers.

Flags

The Mexican flag with its symbol of an eagle with a snake in its mouth, fascinates children. Display a Mexican flag and pictures of flags. Talk about the colors and the symbol on the flag with the children who are interested. Most children are eager to make flags!

To make flags, use fabric or strong white paper such as butcher paper. Make the flags any size a child desires. A suggested size is 8" x 12". Use felt tip markers or crayons to draw and color the symbols. Attach flags to sticks. Let the child use her own creativity in figuring out how to fasten the flag to the stick.

Children's Creative Expression

Children are motivated to express themselves from stories, from resources that give them information about the Mexican cultures, from the things they see in the room and from what the adults tell them about these cultures. They draw and paint pictures of fireworks, dances, bullfights and other experiences from Mexican life.

Cascarones

For Easter the children at the Learning Tree experience one of the traditions of Mexico — cascarones. (Literally translated it means eggshells.)

A cascaron is an empty eggshell that has been painted and filled with colorful confetti. The hole is sealed by gluing tissue paper over it.

Instead of breaking the egg over a bowl, take a knife and cut off just the small end, then shake the contents out. (Needless to say, there will be a lot of scrambled eggs and omelets for the next 2 weeks.)

The children decorate and fill the shells.

The parents hide these cascarones and as the children find them they crack the eggs over the heads of their friends. Don't worry; it doesn't hurt.

This tradition of the cascaron was brought to Mexico from Europe many, many years ago, but the Mexicans and now the Mexican Americans are the only ones who have kept the tradition alive. The coloring inside represents the colors of spring. By releasing the confetti the children release the seasonal colors, much as spring releases us from the bleakness of winter.

Placemats
(Petates)

Placemats or petates are used as table decorations at many Mexican dinners.

Draw pictures or designs on a paper towel or on a plain paper place mat. These mats are available at grocery stores — 100 to a package. Use water base felt tip markers like Draws-a-Lot to make the design. Drip or sprinkle water on the drawings. Watch the colors bleed and run together. Children call this "magic"!

Placemats can also be made by weaving strips of paper of different colors, alternating narrow and wide strips of paper. The woven paper mats look like the Mexican mats.

Cut slits across the length of a piece of construction paper, one or two inches apart. Cut narrow and wide colored strips for weaving. Weave the strips over and under through the slits in the large piece of paper. Staple the ends of the strips to hold them in place.

God's Eye
(Ojo-de-dios)

The God's Eye, a religious object, is a wall hanging. This decoration hangs in many Mexican and Mexican American homes. Some Mexicans believe that the God's Eye wards off evil spirits.

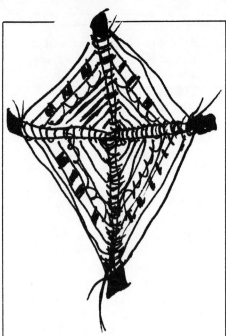

Display books with pictures of mosaic art of Mexico. Display the bold and brilliant style of Mexican artists, such as Alfaro Sequeiros, Diego Rivera and Rufino Tamayo. Bring Mexican pictures from friends or families in your school or in your community. Local museums and libraries may loan pictures.

To make a mosaic, use small pieces and different colors and shapes of construction paper.

Glue pieces of paper close to each other on a sheet of bright-colored construction paper to form a design for a mosaic.

A different effect can be added by painting over the whole mosaic with a solution of one-half water and one-half Elmer's Glue. Place one sheet of colored or white tissue paper on top of the glue before the glue is dry. Mexican American artists include Michael Lopez, Luis Jimenez, Antonio Garcia, Eduardo Carrillo, Mel Casas and Chelo Gonzalez Amerzcua.

To make a God's eye, tie two popsicle sticks together with colored yarn to form a cross. Weave different colors of yarn over and under the sticks, beginning at the center and weaving until the spaces between the sticks are filled and covered. Tie the end of the yarn at the top to make a loop for hanging the God's Eye. Hang on a Christmas tree or in a window. To make a larger God's eye, use longer sticks.

Baskets
(Las Canastas)

Mexican baskets are an artistic contribution by the Mexican cultures. Mexicans weave beautiful designs into their baskets. The beautiful baskets are used in everyday life; for carrying food, clothing and other things. The baskets are important to Mexicans because of their aesthetic quality.

Wrap strong twine or heavy string around a bottle, can or jar. Wrap the jar until it is covered with the twine. Spray or paint with varnish or liquid plastic to give a finish that looks like wicker.

NATURE AND SCIENCE

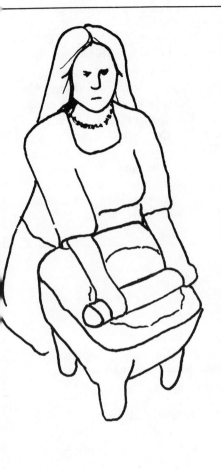

Foods

Some fruits and vegetables native to Mexico are limes, papayas, mangoes, bananas, oranges, avocados, sugar cane, tomatoes, squash and beans. Children may not be familiar with some of the foods. Bring these foods into the classroom. Let children use all of the senses in exploring the foods —feeling, smelling, tasting, seeing and hearing. Talk about the names of the foods and how they grow.

Tropical fruits are often a new experience for children. Using all of their senses to learn about the new fruit, adds to the interest. Bring a papaya —cut, examine and eat. Talk about how the papaya grows. Read about papayas from a children's encyclopedia.

Avocado

Sprinkle the avocado with lime juice and eat.

Guacamole

A dip or salad dressing made from mashed avocado.

Cut avocado in half. Remove seed. Scoop avocado meat from shell. Mash. Add juice from lemon, 1 chopped tomato, salt to taste. Mix. Serve with crisp tortilla chips or use as a salad dressing over raw vegetables.

Plant the avocado seed or put the seed in water. Use toothpicks to hold the seed up so that only the bottom part of the seed is in the water. Watch the avocado leaves grow.

Gum

Sapodilla trees grow in the forests of Mexico. These trees contain chicle which is used for making chewing gum.

Share sugarless gum with children. Talk about how gum is made and how the sugar in the gum affects the teeth.

Sugar Cane

Buy sugar cane at a produce market in season. Children peel off the outer skin and chew the sugar cane. Talk about how sugar is made from sugar cane.

Jumping Beans

The Mexican jumping bean got its name because it jumps from side to side. Its movement is caused by the full grown larva of a moth which lives inside the bean. These beans have value only as a novelty. They are known in Mexico as "leapers".

Break open one or two beans to see the worm inside. Children enjoy playing with the jumping beans. They can be purchased in season at variety stores. Use encyclopedias with the children for more information about jumping beans.

Clay

Mexico is noted for terra-cotta, baked clay. It is used to make dishes and pots.

Use red clay to make pots and other dishes. Buy Mexican red clay from an art supply store. Decorate the moist clay with a sharp object, making designs of flowers and animals.

Clay can be dug from a creek bed and water added to soften it. See the Creative Art Expression section in the chapter on the Native American cultures in this book, for a description of how to prepare clay from a creek bed.

Cactus

Display several different kinds of cacti with books which describe different kinds and uses of cacti.

The fruit and leaves of the prickly pear, a type of cactus, are boiled, fried or stewed, and eaten.

The water stored in the maguey cactus is used by some Mexicans as a drink.

Grow a cactus plant in your room. Observe the small amount of water it takes to keep the cactus alive. Talk about the places in America where many cacti grow.

LANGUAGE DEVELOPMENT

Invite Mexican American parents or other Mexican Americans from the community who are bilingual to talk about how they use two languages. Talk about how most of the children in other countries learn more than two languages in school.

Spanish is used to develop an appreciation for people who speak the language and to interest the English speaking children in learning Spanish words. Children learn some Spanish words, but it is far more important that they learn that people speak languages other than English.

Posters, pictures and books in Spanish and English are available for browsing and reading.

Vocabulary

la casa (la CAH sah) — the house
adobe (a DOH be) — clay brick
amiga (ah MEE gah) — friend, girl
amigo (ah MEE goh) — friend, boy
la familia (la fah MEEL yah) — the family
nino (NEEN yoh) — boy
nina (NEEN yah) — girl
cabeza (cah BEH sah) — head
corazon (coh rah SOHN) — heart
manos (MAH nos) — hands
el libro (el LEE broh) — the book
fiesta (fee ES tah) — party
grande (GRAN deh) — large
atole (ah TOH leh) — a mush made of corn meal
frijoles (free HOLE es) — beans
tortillas (tor TEE yas) — bread
masa (MAH sah) — flour
sombrero (sohm BREH roh) — hat
sarape (sa RAH peh) — blanket
huraches (hu RAH chas) — sandals
los zapatos (los za PAH tohs) — the shoes
rebozo (ra BO zo) — shawl
mantilla (man TE yah) — head scarf

Colors

rojo (ROH hoh) — red
verde (VEHR deh) — green
azul (ah SOOL) — blue
blanco (BLAHN coh) — white
negra (NEH grah) — black
amarilla (ah mah REE yah) — yellow

Conversational Spanish

si (see) — yes
muchas gracias (MOO chas GRAH see has) — thank you
buenos dias (BWEH nohs DEE ahs) — good morning
adios (ah dee OHS) — good-bye
Hola, Como esta usted? (OH lah COH moh ehs TAH oo STED) — Hi, how are you?
me gusta (meh GOOS tah) — I like
Me quieres (meh kee EH rehs) — I want
Me llama (meh YAH mah) — My name is
Por que? (pohr KEH) — Why?
Que? (KEH) — What?
Donde esta? (DOHN DE EHS TAH) — Where is it?

Labeling

Label objects in the room in Spanish and English.

la puerta (la PWEHR tah) — the door
la ventana (la vehn TAH nah) — the window
la silla (la SEE yah) — the chair
la mesa (la MEH sah) — the table
los libros (lohs LEE brohs) — the books

Make word cards with both English and Spanish words on each card. Select words children use often. Either the child copies the word from the word card or the adult prints it for him.

If a child draws a picture of a family in a house, it could be labeled with "la familia" and "la casa" as well as "a family in a house".

Numbers

uno (OO noh) — one
dos (DOHS) — two
tres (TRAYS) — three
cuarto (KWAH troh) — four
cinco (SEEN coh) — five

seis (SAIS)—six
siete (SYAY tah)—seven
ocho (OH choh)—eight
nueve (NWAY vay)—nine
diez (DYES)—ten

Names

Juan (WAN)—John
Andres (ahn DREHS)—Andrew
Antonio (ahn TOH nee oh)—Anthony
Carlos (CAHR lohs)—Charles
Diego (dee AY goh)—James
Pancho (PAHN choh)—Frank
Alicia (ah LEE see ah)—Alice
Ana (AH nah)—Anna
Luisa (loo EE sah)—Louise
Maria (ma REE a)—Mary
Rosa (ROL sa)—Rose

Have a Spanish dictionary in your book center. One example of a dictionary is the Dr. Seuss book, THE CAT IN THE HAT BEGINNER BOOK DICTIONARY IN SPANISH.

Dramatization

Most of the time children provide props they need for their roles in dramatizing stories. Some children need other children to help them find props that satisfy them. The adult has many different things in the room to satisfy the spontaneous needs of the children.

THE STORY OF FERDINAND is available in both Spanish and English. Children dramatize this story over and over again.

Another story about Mexico children enjoy dramatizing is PANCHO.

Spanish Bingo

Mexican Bingo can be purchased in Mexico or in some Mexican import shops.

Make the game by using a picture lotto or bingo game, labeling the pictures with Spanish and English words.

Personal Stories

Experiences from the Mexican cultures give children many ideas for making their own stories. One child dictates a story to an adult who prints it on paper. Some children need encouragement while others will say to the adult, "I made up a story. Please write it while I tell it to you." Children take pride in seeing their own ideas on paper.

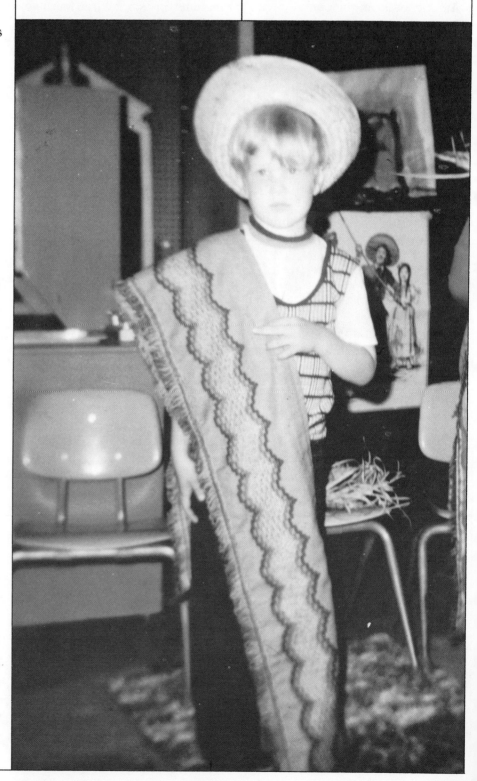

MUSIC AND DANCE

Songs

Buenos Dias
(tune: Happy Birthday)

Buenos dias a ustedes
Buenos dias a ustedes
Buenos dias, buenos dias
Buenos dias a ustedes.

Good Morning

Good morning to you
Good morning to you
Good morning, good morning
Good morning to you.

Feliz Compleanos a Ustedes

Feliz cumpleanos a ustedes
Feliz cumpleanos a ustedes
Feliz cumpleanos (nombre del nino)
Feliz cumpleanos a ustedes.

Happy Birthday to You

Happy birthday to you.
Happy birthday to you.
Happy birthday to (child's name)
Happy birthday to you.

Yo Tengo Gozo

Yo tengo gozol, gozo, gozo, gozo
En mi corazon, en mi corazon, en mi corazon
Yo tengo gozo, gozo, gozo, gozo
En mi corazon, en mi corazon.

I Have a Joy Down in My Heart

I have a joy, joy, joy, joy
Down in my heart, down in my heart, down in my heart.
I have a joy, joy, joy, joy
Down in my heart, down in my heart.

Me Duele la Cabeza

Me duele la cabeza
me duele el corazon
me dule todo el cuerpo
y los dedos de pilon.

My Head Hurts

My head hurts
my heart hurts
all of my body hurts
and even the ends of my
fingers.

Pa- ti -to, pa-ti-to, co-lor de ca-fé, si

tu no me quie- res pues lue-go ¿por qué?

El Patito

Pa-ti-to, pa-ti-to, co-lor de
cafe', si
tu no me quie- res pues lue-
go ¿ por que?

The Little Duck

Little duck, little brown duck,
If you don't like me,
Then please tell me why.

Chants

Tortillitas

Tortillitas, tortillitas,
Tortillitas para Papa.
Tortillitas para Mama.
Tortillitas de salvado
Para Papa, que este enojado.
Tortillitas de manteca
Para Mama, que esta contenta.

Little Patty-Cakes

Little tortillas, little tortillas,
Little tortillas for Papa.
Little tortillas for Mama.
Little tortillas made of bran
For Papa, who is angry.
Little tortillas of lard
For Mama, who is happy.

Recordings

FELIZ NAVIDAD, a
recording by Jose Feliciano, is a
Christmas song.

FRIAR MARTIN, a recording
in the album "Making
Music Your Own", is a song
sung in English and Spanish.

Dance

Children enjoy doing these
dances as a group or
individually. The steps and
movements are simple.

"Mexican Hat Dance"
The national dance of
Mexico (Jarabe Tapatio)

Children make a large circle.
They put one heel forward at
a time to the rhythm of the
music, alternating feet. Then
everyone dances to the right
around the circle. When the
music changes, everyone turns
and dances to the left. Repeat
heels to the rhythm of the
music. Everyone joins hands
and dances to the center of the
circle, raising joined hands
high. Then dance back, forming
a big circle again, bending low.
Repeat 3 times.

La Raspa

Resbale asi su pie,
Uno, dos y tres
Y ahora el otro pie
Uno, dos y tres. (Repeat)

A la derecha, a la derecha
A la derecha, a la derecha
A la izquierda, a la izquierda
A la izquierda, a la izquierda.

Slide your foot this way,
One, two and three
And now the other foot
One, two and three. (Repeat)

To the right, to the right
To the right, to the right
To the left, to the left
To the left, to the left.

Guitar

The guitar is a popular instrument in Mexico. Make a guitar by nailing a wooden cigar box or a foil pan to one end of a 3" x 24" board. Put nails on each end of the board. String rubber bands across the length of the guitar, fastening them to the nails.

Mariachi

Mexico is a land of music. A long time ago, mariaches and marimbas set the mood for the activities of the day.

A mariachi is a group of eight men, dressed in fancy charro suits, who play happy songs. They play marimbas, trumpets and violins with guitar accompaniment. Sometimes, in a restaurant, they walk around to different tables to entertain the guests.

GAMES AND MANIPULATIVES

Bingo

Use a color bingo game and call the colors in Spanish. See Language Development for color words in Spanish.

Lotto

Play picture lotto and number games using Spanish and English. See Language Development for numbers in Spanish.

Puzzles

Play Skool Wood Board Matchups are Matching puzzles using Spanish words.

- People and Their Jobs
- Animals and Their Homes
- Foods and Colors

By Kiersten

SPECIAL EVENTS

Interest Trips

- tortilla factory
- Mexican bakery
- Mexican restaurant
- Mexican import shop
- Trip to farmer's market to buy avocados, papayas, pineapples and sugar cane.
- Watch the newspapers for announcements about local cultural exhibits, Mexican American programs and fiestas in your community.

Mothers Visit

Mexican American mothers visit school to help children make tortillas, tacos, frijoles and guacamole. They also share crafts and other customs from their Mexican American culture.

Mexican Dinner

A dinner for the children of the school and their families is a social and cultural experience. The food is prepared by the teachers, parents and friends. The decorations are from the Mexican and Mexican American cultures. They are planned, created and arranged by the children. The Mexican menu is planned by the teachers and parents. The menu might include:

- enchiladas with chili
- tacos
- refried beans
- rice
- pan dulce

By Noel

El Torero
(The Bullfight)

Children like to dramatize a bullfight. Many characters are needed. One child is El Torro, the bull; another is El Matador, the fighter. Other children are lively spectators—the picatores and the banderilleros. As the Matador challenges the bull by flashing the cape in the bull's view, the bull charges. The Matador is careful never to let the bull's horns touch him.

Holidays

Some holidays celebrated in Mexico, are observed by Mexican Americans in America. Look for announcements in your newspaper of Mexican American holidays celebrated in your community. Take your children to these celebrations or invite some of the parents or leaders of the celebrations to talk to your children about the meaning of the holidays. The following holidays are celebrated in some Mexican American communities.

El Cinco de Mayo
(The Fifth of May)

May 5, 1862 is remembered because Mexican soldiers won over the French army in the Battle of Puebla.

El Dia de la Independencia
(Mexican Independence Day) September 16

A celebration of independence from Spain, won in 1821. On the 15th of September, the mayor of every town in Mexico reads the Declaration of Independence. On the 16th, they have parades and patriotic speeches, and people enjoy the fireworks in the evening.

El Dia de la Raza
(Day of the Race) October 12

This day is celebrated by the Spanish speaking people all over the world, especially in Latin America, to remember their common heritage in language and traditions.

Las Posadas
(The Inn) December 16-24

Groups of Mexican Americans dramatize the story of Mary and Joseph going from inn to inn to find a place to sleep. Activities during this holiday include songs, pinatas, games and refreshments. Christmas is celebrated differently among Mexicans and Mexican Americans depending on the part of the country they are from. But one celebration which seems to be common among most Mexicans and Mexican Americans is the "Posadas".

SELECTED BIBLIOGRAPHY
Mexican American Cultures

BY Demetria

Books for Children

Albaum, Charlet. **Ojo De Dios: Eye of God**. Grosset & Dunlap, 1972.

   This handcraft was borrowed from ancient tradition of Pueblo and Mexican Indians. Gives details for weaving various colored yarns into sticks for the Eye of God. Shapes and designs are mastered by young children.

Archuleta, Nathaniel, dir. **Una Luminaira para Mis Palomitas; El Perrito Perdido; Perlitas de Ayer y Hoy; Ya Perdiste tu Colita, Tita.** Authors: Cecilia Apodaca, Nathaniel Archuleta, Olivia Martinez, Virginia Miera, Felipe Valerio. Distributed by Nathaniel Archuleta, University of New Mexico, 1975.

   Three stories, poems, rhymes and riddles in Spanish and English. Choice of cassette tape or a record with the order of the set of four books.

Belpre, Pura. **Santaigo**. Frederick Warne, 1969.

   Puerto Rican boy seeks to establish relationships in new community. Sensitive friends offer him support. Reflects experience of a minority child. Art by Symeon Shimin adds to the mood of the book.

Bilingual ABC in Verse, ABECEDARIO Bilingue on Verso. Instructional Challenges, 1974.

   In English and Spanish, each letter is accompanied by a verse and suggested activities.

Blue, Rose. **I Am Here, Yo Estoy Aqui**. Franklin Watts, 1971.

   A Puerto Rican child feels lonely in her American environment. Illustrates the importance of bilingual education.

Brenner, Barbara. **Caras (Faces)**. Spanish version by Alma Flor Ada. Dutton, 1977.

   Exploring our faces with photographs and brief text.

Glubok, Shirley. **The Art of Ancient Mexico**. Harper, Row, 1968.

   These photographs of Mexican works of art are a curiosity to children. Similar clay and pottery figures may be viewed in local museum.

Hader, Berta. **Pancho**. Macmillan, 1942.

   Pancho shows how to cope with fear. Illustrations give personality to animals and people.

Krumgold, Joseph. **And Now Miguel**. Apollo, 1970.

Miguel has a strong desire to go with the men to take the sheep to summer pasture. Film available from Universal-Education and Visual Arts.

Leaf, Munro. **The Story of Ferdinand**. Viling Press, 1936.

Children enjoy this story. Leads to dramatic play with children taking parts of banderlleras, picadores and matadores. Available in Spanish, **El Cuento de Ferdinande**.

Marcus, Rebbecca B. and J. **Fiesta Time in Mexico**. Garrard, 1974.

Excellent photographs of the nacimento, posado, and numerous celebrations of interest to young children. Serves as a resource for adults and children.

Nims, Bonnie. **Yo Quisiera Vivir en un Parque de Jegos: I Wish I Lived at the Playground**. Translated by Ramon S. Ocellana. O'Hara Publishers, 1972.

Spanish/English Chicano, Black and White children enjoy the freedom a playground allows.

Rockwell, Anne F. **El Torro Pinto and Other Songs in Spanish**. Macmillan, 1971.

Songs reflect the mood of Mexico. Language is Spanish but rhythms and melodies are of many cultures. Translations.

Serfozo, Mary. **Welcome, Roberto!: Bienvenido, Roberto!** Follett, 1969.

The setting for this story is an informal integrated classroom.

Dr. Seuss. **The Cat in the Hat Beginner Book Dictionary in Spanish**. Beginner. 1966.

Excellent reference book for Spanish words.

Simon, Norma. **What Do I Say?: i Que Digo?** Whitman, 1967.

An English/Spanish version with large pictures and brief text, includes basic greetings which are helpful for learning either English or Spanish.

The children at the Learning Tree also enjoy the following books. Look for them in your library.

Carlson, Vada F., **High Country**
Cooper, Lee, **Fun With Spanish**
Dines, Glen, **Sun, Sand and Steel: Costumes and Equipment of the Spanish Mexican Southwest**
Goldberg, Martha, **Big House, Little House**
Grifalconi, Ann, **The Toy Trumpet**
Guis, Darlene, **Let's Travel in Mexico**
Hampton, Doris, **Just for Manuel**
Hood, Flora, **One Luminaria for Antonio**
Tood, Barbara, **Juan Patricio**
Vavra, Robert, **Pizorro**
When We Go To Market, Cuando Vamos al Mercado

Books for Adults

Castanéda, Alfredo and others, **New Approaches to Bilingual, Bicultural Education**, 1975, Bilingual Resource Center, 7703 North Lamar, Austin, TX 78752.

Recommended methods for working with children. Independent self-paced instruction is suggested.

Corbitt, Helen, **Mexico Through my Kitchen Window**. Houghton Mifflin, 1961.

Translation of a Mexican cookbook. Special section on foods for Mexican holidays. Hints for Texan Mexican recipes, how to adapt them for people north of the border.

Dunn, Lynn P. **Chicanos: A Study Guide and Sourcebook**. R & E, 1975.

Simple topical study guide about the history and conflicts of the Chicano in America to 1971. Also additional references.

Information and Materials to Teach the Cultural Heritage of the Mexican American Child, 1974, Bilingual Resource Center, 7703 North Lamar, Austin, TX 78752.

Source of authentic background information and materials. Includes stories and legends, music, dances, celebrations. All areas of the Mexican American cultures. Excellent source.

Marcus, Rebecca B. and J. **Fiesta Time in Mexico**. Garrard, 1974.

Describes Mexican traditions and celebrations.

McWilliams, Carey. **Mexicans in America**. Teachers College, 1968.

History of Mexican Americans and the conflict among cultures in the southwest.

National Clearinghouse for Bilingual Education, 1300 Wilson Blvd., Suite B2-11, Rosslyn, VA 22209.

Write for list of publications on bilingual education.

Paredes, Americo. **Mexican American Authors**. Houghton Mifflin, 1972.

Anthology of folklore by Mexican American authors and selections from their literature during the last fifty years.

Prieto, Mariana, col. **Play It in Spanish**. John Day, 1973. Music by E.C. Nielsen.

Spanish games and folk songs for children in English and Spanish for children. From several Hispanic countries.

Quirarte, Jacinto, **Mexican American Artists**. University of Texas, 1973.

Visual art shows the culture authentically.

Sandoval, Ruben and D. Strick. **Games, Games, Games; Juego, Juegos, Chicano Children at Play – Games and Rhymes**. Doubleday, 1977.

Through many photographs and text authors describe the complex play of Chicano children. All kinds of games they have played for many years.

Schon, Isabel, **A Hispanic Heritage**, Scarecrow, 1980.

An annotated guide to juvenile books about Hispanic people and cultures – of Spain, and Latin and Central American countries. Author evaluates authenticity of books.

Weiner, Sandra, **Small Hands, Big Hands**, profiles of Chicano migrant workers and their families. Pantheon, 1970.

About Mexican migrant families. Full-page photographs.

Willes, Burlington, **Games and Ideas for Teaching Spanish**, Pitman Learning, 1967.

Source for learning Spanish, especially for the primary grades.

Magazines

Americas
Monthly
General Secretariat, Organization of American States, Sales and Promotion Division, Washington, DC 20006.

About cultures of Latin American countries in the Western hemisphere. Many illustrations are in color. Articles about countries, natural resources, cultures, literature, history and folk art. In English, Spanish and Portuguese.

Bilingual Review / Revista Bilingue
Three issues a year
Department of Foreign Languages, York College of the City University of New York, Jamaica, NY 11451.

Covers English-Spanish bilingualism in the United States. Reviews successful bilingual educational programs and reviews new publications. Also has Chicano and Puerto Rican poetry, short stories and articles about personalities. In English and Spanish.

Nuestro
Monthly
Nuestro Publications Inc., 1140 Avenue of Americas, New York, NY 10036.

Magazine for latinos – Cubans, Mexicans and Puerto Ricans. Wide variety of articles including arts, personalities and short stories. A well-illustrated publication. In English with Spanish summaries.

Records and Films

A Taste of Education: Building Your Spanish Vocabulary Through Music. Read by Eddie Cano. C.P. Records, Inc., 7291 Pacific View Drive, Los Angeles, CA 90028.
Record CP100

A teacher presents this excellent method of teaching English to Spanish-speaking children and Spanish to children whose first language is English. Children learn vocabulary by repeating Cano's statements.

"Fray Martin" with Alice Girgau. **Making Music Your Own**. Album 6 records. Silver Burdett Company. Dist: General Learning Corporation, 8301 Ambassador Road, Dallas, TX 75247.
Album 75180

Children learn song in English and Spanish. They dramatize "tan tan tan tan". Book accompanies album.

"La Raspa" with Ella Jenkins. **Little Johnny Brown**. One record. Folkways Records. Dist: Scholastic Records, 906 Sylvan, Englewood Cliffs, NJ 07632. Record SC7631

An instrumental record of this famous traditional dance. Ella Jenkins is an expert in involving children in movement.

"Mexican Hand Clapping Chant" with Ella Jenkins. **Little Johnny Brown**. One record. Folkways Records. Dist: Scholastic Records, address above. Record SC7631

Children enjoy participating in the song. An enjoyable way to learn Spanish.

"Villa Alegre". Prod. Bilingual Children's Television (BC/TV). 30 minutes weekly.

Series about Juanito, a six-year-old, as he experiences a cultural shock. Objectives are to create an awareness of and respect for other lifestyles and cultural differences, and to bring ethnic communities closer together.

By Tico

Native American Cultures

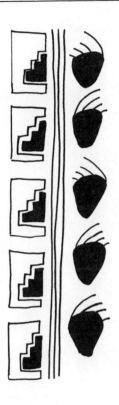

Young children learn that there are many different Native groups and that each group has different customs and traditions. Children learn to say Sioux, Hopi, and Apache as easily as Native American or Indian. Native people live in cities, towns and reservations. Some Native Americans participate in traditional ways and others do not.

An effort has been made in this chapter to explain what Native groups did "a long time ago" and what they experience in the modern world. Children learn that Indians are not people who belong to the past.

FAMILY LIVING

Homes

Long ago family living was different for each Native group. The Iroquois and groups who lived in the woodland areas made longhouses of poles covered with bark. The Hopi adobe, the Navajo hogan, the Kickapoo wigwam, the Cherokee chickee and the Iroquois longhouse are interesting to young children.

Today some Native groups live in these houses while others do not live on reservations or in rural areas. They have moved to cities and towns. The modern house of the Kickapoos in Coahuila looks like the early wigwam. Other Kickapoos have frame houses and some have wigwams that are now covered, not with bark, but with mats and canvas. The Eastern pueblos in New Mexico have adobe houses built around plazas. The Hopi masonry pueblo-type towns are on top of the mesas. Today the hogan is used by some Navajos.

Unfortunately, at the beginning of a Native American awareness week, young children recall these television stereotypes. Adults help them understand that the Native American groups have many languages and cultures. Do not encourage "Cowboys and Indians" and do not use "Wild Indians". A stereotype means repeating the same idea or image. If a child sees only the plains Indian with headband and feather, she believes that all Native groups are like that. Help parents be sensitive to stereotypes and to discuss the television programs their children watch.

The most common of all stereotypes is the feathered headdress, the horseman collecting scalps and the war hoop of the Plains Indians. This stereotype has come to symbolize all Native groups.

paint and stack the boxes, large ones on the bottom to make the pueblo several stories high. Make ladders by gluing popsicle sticks together. Some children draw and cut people which they add to the village.

Sioux Tipi

Today the Sioux live in frame houses like other rural Dakotans or in log cabins. Traditional tipis appear only in connection with summer ceremonials and religious rites. The Native groups who lived in buffalo country used a tent for shelter when they hunted. Sometimes they decorated the tent with designs of circles, squares, triangles and straight lines. The tipi was ideal for groups who moved from place to place because it could easily be taken down and set up again in the next hunting area.

Make a tent or tipi by stretching old sheets or any type of covering over a frame. The tent gives children a chance to experience the cozy atmosphere of a tipi with a fireplace and with beds on the ground. Tipis are available in the toy section of some department stores.

Hopi Pueblo Adobe

The Pueblo groups were the first multi-storied "apartment builders". Most of the adobes or houses are built in the old step design, with each floor set back by the depth of one room from the front of the floor below it. The style of the adobe served as a protection and for comfort. Ladders were used to reach the different stories.

Use different sizes of boxes. Paint the boxes with brown

Cherokee Chickee

The Learning Tree has a treehouse in its school. The children add grasses to the roof and sides to make it a house with a thatched roof. The house is called a chickee. This type of house was used by the Cherokee Tribe of Florida and by the Alabama-Coushatta Tribe in Texas.

Iroquois Longhouse

Make an Iroquois longhouse out of a large cardboard box. Children play in the house, pretending to lie on the bunks and to cook fish on the fires, which are in the middle of the longhouse.

Another way to involve the children in role play is to paint very large cardboard boxes and use them as a larger adobe. The children can get into these houses.

An excellent place to visit is the Hopi Cultural Center, located on State Highway 264 between Tuba City and Keams Canyon on Second Mesa. A modern motel, designed like the adobe with restaurant, museum, arts and crafts, and conference room, is centrally located to the Hopi Villages. To make reservations for the motel call (602) 734-2401.

Clothing

Some Native Americans wear traditional clothing some of the time. Traditional clothing is also worn at ceremonial times.

Have clothing and objects available for use in role-playing family life.

- headdresses
- shirts
- moccasins
- long dresses
- beads
- long full skirts
- shields
- coup sticks
- bows

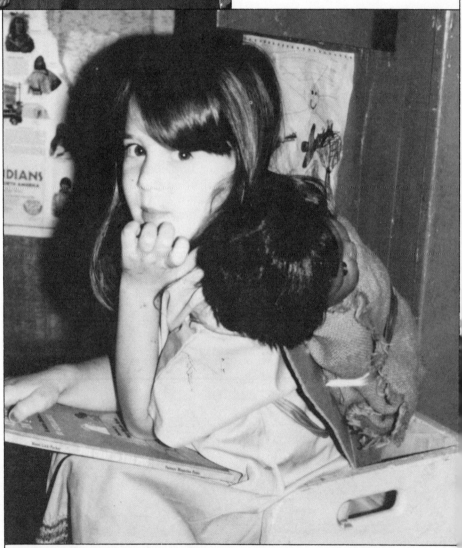

Apache Cradleboards

Provide cradleboards and dolls to carry as babies.

Instructions for making them are in this section.

part of the life of the Native groups. The staff from the Learning Tree participated in a workshop at Oraibi, Arizona. As a result of the workshop, the staff is now aware that traditional foods are no longer served on a daily basis, but they are prepared and eaten only on special days.

At the workshop the group parched corn, made Blue Fry Bread, Blue Marbles, Blue Corn Meal Pudding and Roasted Piki.

One Hopi woman made piki bread. She mixed boiling water, blue corn meal and cooking ashes and spread it over a hot stone. She rolled it and served the crisp and tissue thin piki. The woman did not bake piki bread every day. She did this for a special occasion for the workshop. Usually she cooks in a more modern way.

Making piki bread is handed down by the man or woman doing the cooking.

An excellent cookbook to use with young children is PUEBLO AND NAVAJO COOKERY by Marcia Keegan.

Ojibwa (Chippewa) Canoe

Many Native groups used canoes made of bark. Canoe making among the Chippewa is supervised by an expert; the men do the woodwork and the women sew.

Children can make a canoe from a large box. They paint the canoe and decorate it with designs. Each Native group has special symbols that are important to their culture.

Foods and Cooking Experiences

Any experience that includes the sense of taste, adds more meaning to the development of that concept for the young child.

Some Native groups planted corn, baked clams, and baked beans by burying pots of beans in the ground. Other groups made corn pone, used seaweed for fertilizer, and grew pumpkins and squash.

Some of the foods which can be cooked in a classroom are:

- cornbread
- corn-on-the-cob
- popcorn
- cranberries
- peanuts
- sweet potatoes
- roasted pumpkin seeds

It is very important to understand that many traditional ways are no longer a

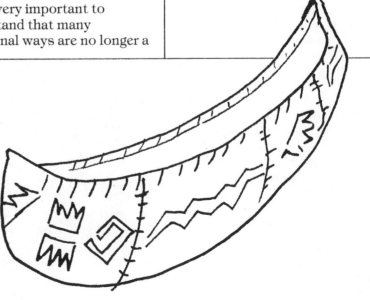

7. Fry the dough in hot oil until the edges are browned on both sides.

Blue fry bread may be eaten with salt or honey on it. It is usually served with beans or stew.

The corn grown on the Hopi reservation comes in many colors. The dark blue corn is ground and Someviki (soe-me-vee-kee) is made by adding ashes (qoots-vee) that are made by burning dry corn cobs, dried leaves, stems, and pods of bean plants.

Hopi people preparing dishes do not use recipes. Because they learn how to cook during childhood, they also learn how the ingredients feel and look. The teachers at the Learning Tree adapted the Hopi recipe and make it the following way.

Fry Bread

1 cup flour
2 teaspoons baking powder
½ teaspoon salt
¾ cup milk

Mix ingredients together, adding more flour if necessary to make a stiff dough. Roll out on a floured board until it is very thin. Cut into strips, about two or three inches long and one inch wide. Drop into hot oil. Brown on both sides. Serve hot with butter or sprinkle with sugar. This recipe makes about 10 servings.

Hopi Blue Fry Bread
(sak-wa-wee-oe-qa-vee-kee)

About 2½ cups of flour
About 1/3 cup of blue corn meal
About 1 tablespoon baking soda
About 1 teaspoon salt
About 2 cups of water
lard or cooking oil

1. Put flour in a large bowl. Add about a handful of blue cornmeal, a little salt and baking powder. A small amount of powdered milk may or may not be added.

2. Mix the dry ingredients well.

3. Gradually add water, a little at a time, mixing with your hands as you add it. Keep doing this until you have a soft and pliable dough.

4. Let the dough set for about an hour before frying time.

5. Form a small ball of dough for each piece of fry bread.

6. Roll out the dough balls with a rolling pin to about ½ inch thick.

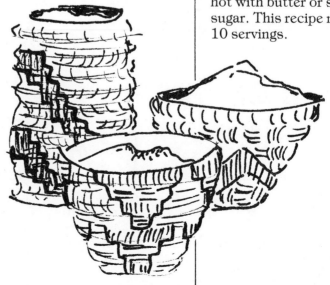

CREATIVE ART EXPRESSION

Headdress

With imagination and materials, a child can wear a headdress. Colors for headdress are the natural color of turkey or eagle feathers, dark brown.

Children can make headdresses several ways.

- Fold one page of a newspaper horizontally to make band. Decorate with Indian designs and with paper feathers made by the children.

- Use fabric strips for bands. Decorate band with felt markers and add paper feathers.

- Make band of corrugated cardboard. Decorate and use paper or real feathers, if available. Turkey feathers are available at turkey farms or long feathers can be purchased at craft stores.

Cradleboards

Babies carried in cradleboards made of soft moss-lined beds of wood and

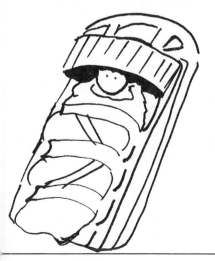

The resourcefulness of the Native American, who at one time made everything he needed, inspires young children to make the things they need and want to use instead of buying them. Today some Native people use the old hand tools along with modern implements.

animal hide. Children will carry boards with a supportive strap across the forehead, a tampline, or with straps over their shoulders.

Make cradleboards by cutting a piece of cardboard, 12" x 18", the size of the doll. Punch holes on each side of cardboard, about 3 holes on each side. Place doll on cardboard. Lace strips of cloth through the holes and crisscross over the doll to hold it onto the board. Tie ends of strips to make tampline or tie strips into loops which fit over shoulders.

Shirts / Skirts

Some Native women wore half-length skirts made of deerskin with streamers of buckskin hanging from the bottom of the skirt. Ceremonial shirts were worn by Native Americans from all tribes.

Parents can make shirts and skirts. Children draw designs on the clothing with felt markers. Use water-based markers so that the clothing can be washed and used again.

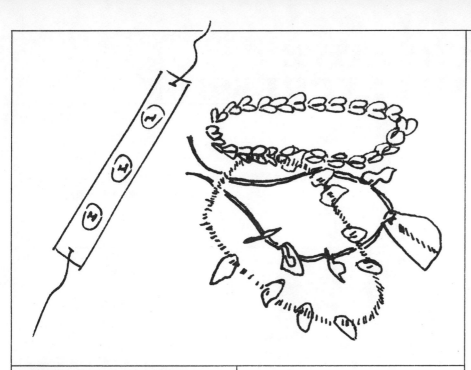

Bows

Bows of yew and other hard woods were often decorated.

To make bows, gather sticks from the outdoors. When a child finds an appropriate stick for the bow, she strings it and fastens twine to each end of the stick. Skin of the neck of a snapping turtle was used by the Indians. Children use twine instead of skin.

Arrows

Woodland Indians made arrows of wood with an arrowhead of stone.

Make arrows from sticks. Attach a small pointed rock to the stick with masking tape. Arrows can also be made from 1" x 12" strips of heavy cardboard. Traingles made of construction paper may be attached for arrowheads.

Use any type of cardboard tube for the case in which the bow and arrow are kept. The case can also be made from heavy paper. Roll the paper and form a tube from an 11" x 18" peice of construction paper. Cover one end with masking tape. Fasten strip of fabric or leather with masking tape to make a strap for carrying the case.

Mandan Arrow Quiver

Mandans made their arrow quivers out of buffalo hide.

A good target for these "dangerous weapons" is a large picture of a buffalo or other animal. Encourage children to draw large animals. Paint, color and cut out the animal, then tape it to a wall.

Masks

Children change into the spirit of the Native American by putting on a mask.

Jewelry

Indians made beads from shells, bones, claws, stones and minerals. Holes were drilled in small shells and then strung. Pueblo groups made necklaces with clam shells strung with turquoise or coral. Children make bracelets, necklaces and beads, stringing the following:

- shells
- metal disks
- macaroni that has been dyed
- colored plastic straws cut into short pieces
- bones from meat, like bones from ham and round steak
- different shapes of colored paper with a hole punched in the middle

String items on colored yarn. For easier stringing, wrap one end of yarn with masking tape.

Armbands

Indians use armbands as a part of their ceremonial dress. Armbands worn on the upper arm often add the effect a child needs as he plays the role of the Native American.

Make ankle and armbands with jingle bells strung or tied to leather strips. Leather strips are inexpensive and can be purchased in quantity at sporting goods stores. Cloth may be used instead of leather.

Mohave Bows

Indians used bows and arrows, spears, tomahawks, clubs and knives to hunt bear, buffalo and other large animals.

These disguises are made from paper or cardboard. Add features of the face by gluing colored yarn, pieces of cloth and other collage materials to the mask. Children wear their masks when they perform the "tribal dances". The inhibited child feels more free and relaxed when she wears a false face. LITTLE RUNNER OF THE LONGHOUSE is a story about a custom using the Native American mask.

Totem Poles

Haidas were famous for their totem poles and house posts. They displayed decorated poles with carved crests outside their homes. The totem poles usually told a legend or some story about the family.

All sizes of cardboard boxes, painted by children, make colorful decorated "trees" or totem poles. Each child may draw a picture on the side of a box. The picture may be an animal, a scene or any Indian design.

An adult and child can tell tales when stacking the boxes to make a totem pole. Figures of animals, people and fish illustrate the story. The finished totem pole adds a cultural spirit to the room.

Pottery

The Pueblo groups are known for their pottery. The culture of a group can be traced from the designs on its pottery. Pueblo artists make pottery into very beautiful shapes.

A good place for natural clay is to dig it from a creek bed. Children enjoy the outings to dig for clay, then to dry it, pound it and to pull out the things in the clay, like stones.

Add water to the clay and knead it. Preparing the clay is an important activity for motor development and for sensory experiences. This activity helps children understand how the Native Americans made pottery out of clay.

Some children shape crude storage jars, canteens, bowls and cooking pots out of the clay.

Feather Painting

Feather painting gives an unusual effect. Use feathers as paint brushes. Materials from nature are recycled in this activity.

Picture Skin Story

Long ago some Native Americans used picture writing to express thoughts or to record history. These picture-skin stories were written on tanned skins in the shape of a circle beginning in the center of the skin. Some of the picture-skin stories told about exciting hunting trips.

Picture writing was highly developed by the Chippewa. Crush brown wrapping paper to give an animal-skin look. Draw Indian symbols on the crushed paper to make a picture-skin story.

Navajo Weaving

The Navajo Indians are famous weavers of blankets. Their designs often tell stories.

Set up a frame so that children can weave for short periods of time. Children make small frames by hammering nails into boards. Instructions for weaving are in the section on Music and Dance in this chapter.

Cheyenne Coup Sticks

Long ago coup sticks were trophies or symbols of bravery of a warrior. Each feather on the coup stick represented a brave deed the warrior had done.

Children can make coup sticks. Use a 36" stick. Attach a strip of 1" x 24" leather or fabric to the stick. Tape paper or real feathers, or staple them along the strip.

Sandpainting

Some Native Americans believe that a circle painted in sand spirits illnesses away from them. The value for young children may be in knowing that other people have different beliefs and in appreciating sandpainting as an art form.

Things having to do with Native religion should not be taught in the classroom. When children view pictures of sandpainting they talk about how it is done, the colors and as the young child in the picture, try out the experience in the sand.

Another religious ceremony is the Kachina dance. The Kachina dolls are beautiful to children. Do not have children imitate this ceremony by trying to carve this doll, since this imitation is very offensive to many Hopi families.

Rock Painting

Native Americans are in harmony with nature, people and animals. Young children delight in collecting rocks, branches, and other items from nature.

Children paint rocks of different sizes with a mixture of thin tempera paint.

Crow Shield

As a young "Indian" ventured into the unknown, he took his shield with "magic powers" for protection. Each Native group used a different shape and design for a shield. Crow shields were made from the heavy skin of a buffalo's neck.

A display of pictures of shields helps a child decide on the shape, style and design for the shield he chooses to make. The same materials used for masks may be used to decorate the shields. Attach a piece of elastic, rubber band or string for carrying it.

Mural

Murals illustrate the different types of places where the Native Americans lived. Use books for illustrations and information on the different kinds of homes and environment of the different groups. Many books are listed in the bibliography.

Children draw and paint mountains, trees, rocks, rivers, animals and many other things. Use murals as a backdrop to suggest the environment of the different tribes. Print the names of each group on the mural.

NATURE AND SCIENCE

Display

A display of natural materials shows how resourceful some Native Americans are. Some materials are used for religious purposes and others for hunting.

Children touch, see and examine materials from nature.

- dried Indian corn
- rocks
- feathers, bones, skin and skulls of cattle
- deer, squirrels and dogs.

Dyeing

Berries, fruits, vegetables and leaves were used by Native Americans for dyeing cloth.

Cut raw vegetables and fruits into pieces and rub them against the cloth. Experiment with a variety of fruits and vegetables. Try blueberries, beets and leaves. The juice of some of the vegetables and fruits can be used to paint on fabric with a brush. The liquid from boiled onions makes a yellow color. To dye the cloth place it in the onion liquid for about fifteen minutes. Hang to dry.

Dissolve red clay in water and paint with it.

THE INDIANS KNEW is a valuable book for science experiments about air and smoke, floating objects, drying food, dyeing cloth, sound, and campfires.

When using the ideas from this book, explain to the

Many Native Americans are ecologists. They preserve the natural environment. They use the resources in the land wisely. They care about keeping the balance in nature and show an understanding of the relationship between themselves and their surroundings. Many Native Americans adapt to their environment instead of changing it.

children that Indians did these things a long time ago. Help the children to think about the Native groups as being a part of the modern world and not only people of the past.

LANGUAGE DEVELOPMENT

Vocabulary

The following words are used in labeling pictures and objects in the room. This is a suggested list; other words may be added.

adobe
Alabama-
  Coushatta
brave
buffalo
canoe
Cherokee
coup stick
Crow
desert
forest
Iroquois
Kickapoo
moccasin

Navajo
Papagos
Pima
plains
pottery
pow-wow
quiver
shield
Sioux
tipi
totem pole
wampum
wigwam
woodlands

Do not allow children to say "Ugh" and "how". They hear the authentic languages recorded on some of the records in the bibliography.

A majority of Native groups continue to speak a Native language in addition to English. Many others use words of their Native language when referring to things that are part of their cultural heritage.

Stories

Children dictate stories using words and ideas suggested by their Native American experiences and activities.

Display large posters with Indian symbols matched with English words. Some children copy these symbols and print a message.

Many books and pictures should be available to acquaint young children with the Native American cultures. The stories and pictures encourage new language.

Symbols

tribe

lake

canoe

canoe with people

walking

forest

many

lightning

man

woman

cactus

bear track

rattlesnake jaw

mountain

paths crossing

peace

home

time

Folktales

Folktales make little sense if not given the background of the life of the people who originally told them.

Stories and tales are still told to children in many Native groups at home and at school.

Non-Indians enjoy the interesting characters, the adventure, and the animals who talk and who do what people do.

Dramatization

Children usually find props they need for dramatizing stories. Some children need help in deciding on props that satisfy them. Have a variety of materials available for props which can be used for many stories. Many items in the classroom, like blocks, are used for many different kinds of props.

Favorite stories for dramatization:

- LITTLE RUNNER OF THE LONGHOUSE
- POCAHONTAS
- SALT BOY
- THUNDERBIRD: AN INDIAN LEGEND
- NAVAJO PET

Navajo Prayer

Learn the Navajo prayer for departing. Children learn this prayer easily. Motions may be added to the prayer.

Hogooneh – So be it

There shall be happiness before us.
(Arms stretched in front)

There shall be happiness behind us.
(Arms stretched behind body)

There shall be happiness above us.
(Arms stretched above head)

There shall be happiness below us.
(Bend and touch the floor)

There shall be happiness all around us.
(Turn around with arms spread out)

Words of happiness shall extend from our mouths.
(Touch lips with both hands and stretch arms outward)

MUSIC AND DANCE

Dance

The basis for dances came from the daily life of the Native Americans. They celebrated corn harvest, worshipped the sun and rain, and they dramatized war.

Shield Dance

The shield dance was a war dance.

Children must have a shield for the Shield Dance. Children create their own shields. Instructions for making shields are in the section on Creative Art Expression in this chapter.

Hoop Dance

The Hoop Dance is a dance performed by some of the Pueblo groups in New Mexico.

A small hoola hoop is used by the children to perform this dance. The child holds the hoop and puts one leg in and alternates legs in and out the hoop.

Discuss with non-Indian children how Native groups have very special and planned steps to be used with each dance.

A resource person from the Indian Center came to the Learning Tree and described the steps, teaching the children that Native people do not just

Long ago Native Americans had ceremonial dances to ask their gods for rain and for good harvests. These dances were different in each group. Many ceremonial dances have been revived and are being learned again.

jump up and down to music.

INDIAN SONGS OF THE SOUTHWEST is authentic music. See the bibliography for information about this recording.

Pow-Wow

The word pow-wow was a term used by the Algonquian Tribe. Pow-wow meant that tribes were coming together to dance and to acknowledge their common bonds.

Although the Indians only participate in the pow-wows once or twice a year, young children come together frequently for a pow-wow. It is a special time to perform dances, to sing, to tell stories and to share experiences about Native Americans.

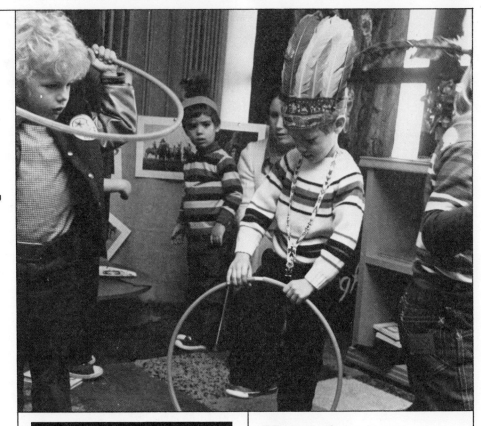

Songs

Recordings of Native American songs listed in the bibliography are:
- INDIAN SONGS OF THE SOUTHWEST
- SHEE-NASHA
- SOUNDS OF INDIAN AMERICA: PLAINS AND SOUTHWEST

The songs on these recordings appeal to children.

Musical Instruments

Musical instruments were used by the Native groups to furnish rhythm for the dancers.

Children use instruments they have made to accompany their dances.

Moraches

Moraches add to the music making. Moraches are notched sticks rubbed against another stick or a bone. Rub the moraches on a hollow gourd or on a box for a resonant sound.

Rattles

Use baking powder cans for rattles. Make rattles by filling the tin cans one-fourth full with small stones. Decorate the outside of the can.

Make rattles for legs by stringing bottle caps, shells or bells.

Drums

Drums were made from tree trunks with skin from animals stretched over the open ends.

Make drums from coffee cans or oatmeal boxes. Children may suggest other materials.

GAMES AND MANIPULATIVES

Games

Games were the most popular recreation of the Native Americans. Today traditional games are not played often but they are played on ceremonial days.

- **Hidden ball game**—played the same as "Button, Button, Who's Got the Button?"
- **Relays, tag games, hide and seek**—described in GAMES OF THE AMERICAN INDIAN by Baldwin, listed in the bibliography.
- **Lotto**—game with Indian symbols for pictures.

Manipulatives

- **Puzzles** with authetnic Native American pictures.
- **Small beads** for sorting, string, counting.
- **Wooden beads** for stringing, sorting into groups of different sizes.
- **Nuts** of different kinds for sorting, describing and eating.

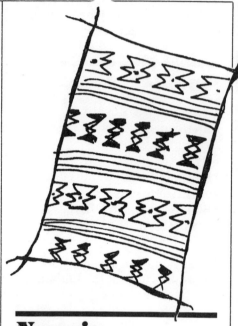

Navajo Weaving

Make a large wooden loom from 36" dowels. Use as a loom for weaving. Have a basket of long strips of fabric and yarn for weaving available. This is an on-going project. Children sit on the floor and weave, imitating the Navajos. Use the woven "artistic" product as a wall hanging.

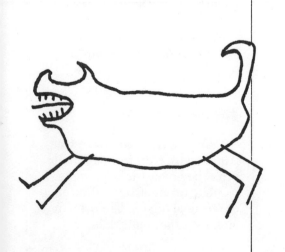

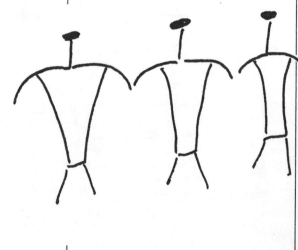

SPECIAL EVENTS

Interest Trips and Resources

Children gain an awareness of the Native American tribes from resource persons, interest trips and outings.

- Visit Indian school
- Invite Indian children to visit your school
- Invite resource persons from the Indian Center in your community to talk to children and to bring authentic artifacts

- Identify resources for Native American tribes in your community. Inquire at the public library, Chamber of Commerce and local organizations, for Native American speakers

- Visit Indian reservation if it is near to your community.

Harvest Feast

Children plan and prepare the food for the feast. They arrange and set the tables. Families and friends are invited to share in this feast. Menu might include:

- meatballs
- rabbit
- corn-on-cob
- fruits
- cranberries
- biscuits

Special Days

These events are celebrated by some of the Native American tribes.

American Indian Day
September 26
(Dates change, fourth Friday in September)

Many schools have special events about the history of the Native Americans in North America.

Indian Day of Glory
June 25

The Plains Tribe protected their hunting grounds and way of life for many years. On this day many years ago, Custer was killed—a victory for the Sioux and Cheyenne Tribes.

All American Indian Days
August 3-6

During the first week in August, many Native American tribes gather in Sheridan, Wyoming to celebrate All American Indian Days and the Miss Indian American Pageant.

Inter-Tribal Indian Ceremonial
August 17-20
(dates change)

Each year Gallup, New Mexico is the scene of the Inter-Tribal Ceremonial. It features some 500 Indian dancers from many Native American tribes in authentic costumes.

Hopi Snake Dance
August 23-26
(dates change)

The Snake Dance is the most famous ceremonial of the Hopi Tribe. This dance is the prayer for rain. Usually, it is held in August, but the medicine men do not decide on the exact dates until 16 days before the ceremony.

Thanksgiving

Traditional Thanksgiving celebrations in schools often use stereotypes of Native Americans and of the history of the United States. The editors of the **Interracial Books for Children Bulletin** have included articles on celebrating Thanksgiving in two issues of their bulletin. The two articles are: "Celebration or Mourning?" (Vol. 10, No. 4) and "Why I'm Not Thankful for Thanksgiving" (Vol. 9, No. 7). The address for this bulletin is in the last chapter of this book.

The concepts which should be considered in planning a Thanksgiving celebration include: how Native Americans helped Pilgrams live in America, how Pilgrams and other Europeans destroyed almost all Native Americans in New England, how many children's books give a false picture of the Native Americans and why many Native Americans today consider Thanksgiving as a day of mourning.

The celebration of Thanksgiving, IF it is to include Native Americans, must emphasize an appreciation of all Native American tribes as they were, and as they are, today.

SELECTED BIBLIOGRAPHY
Native American Cultures

Books for Children

Albaum, Charlet. **Ojo De Dios: Eye of God**. Grosett & Dunlap, 1972.

This handcraft was borrowed from ancient tradition of Pueblo and Mexican Indians. Details for weaving various colored yarns for Eye of God. Many shapes and designs are mastered by young children.

Aliki. **Corn Is Maize: The Gift of the Indians**. Crowell, 1976.

Communicating a number of valuable ideas to children, this non-fiction book explores relationships between people and nature, interdependence between people, facts about corn.

Allen, Terry, ed. **The Whispering Wind: Poetry by Young Indians**. Doubleday, 1972.

Introduce the poem "Celebration" by Aloza Lopez and "Dancing Tepees" by Calvin John.

Baker, Betty. **Little Runner of the Longhouse**. Harper & Row, 1962.

An "I Can Read" book with descriptive illustrations by Arnold Lobel.

Children identify with young Indian as he "tricks or treats" in Indian tradition in Iroquois New Year's ceremonies.

Baylor, Byrd. **When Clay Sings**. Scribner's Sons, 1972.

Text speaks of reverence for bits of clay. "They say that every piece of clay is a piece of someone's life"—this sets the mood for the text. Illustrations by Tom Banti are of black, brown and cream combination and complement the story written by an Indian author. Gives children an appreciation for pottery as a link in history.

Brindze, Ruth. **The Story of the Totem Pole**. Vanguard Press, 1951.

Describes how Northwest Coast Indians used poles for their story-telling records. Adapted for young children. Provides material that may initiate creation of totem poles.

Claiborne, Robert. **The First Americans**. Time Life, 1973.

Offers insight into the history and rich cultural background of the Eskimos, Northwest Indians, Southwest Indians, and the Mound Builders. Photographs and drawings add to the book.

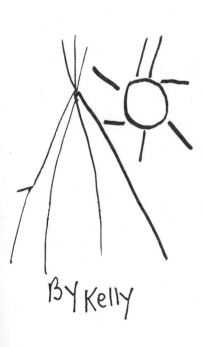

By Kelly

By Kumiko

Cody, Iron Eyes. **Indian Sign Talk In Pictures**. Boelter Classics, 1953.

Booklet is used to learn to communicate by signs. No distinction made about signs for individual tribes. Young children learn signs and create new ones. Importance of non-verbal communication is inferred.

Crowder, Jack L. **Stezanii doo Ma'll**. Jack L. Crowder, 1969, Box 278, Bernalillo, New Mexico 87004.

Bilingual text relates adventure of Stephanii, a young Navajo girl, in search of her goat. Designed to enable Navajos to read in their own language. Copies of booklet available from the author.

Clymer, Theodore. **Four Corners of the Sky: Poems, Charts and Oratory**. Little, Brown, 1975.

Expressions of hope and despair from numerous Indian cultures. Young children appreciate the bold color illustrations by Marc Brown.

D'Amato, Janet and Alex. **Indian Crafts**. Lion Press, 1968.

Book of crafts recognizes the skill and creative talents of the Native American. Pueblo dwelling, war bonnet, ceremonial club and drums are among the handcrafts especially appealing to young children.

Friskey, Margaret. **Indian Two Feet and His Horse**. Scholastic, 1964.

The wish for a horse of his own comes true. One in a series about Indian Two Feet. Sensitive illustrations by Ezra Jack Keats.

Glubok, Shirley. **The Art of the North American Indian**. Harper & Row, 1964.

Museum photographs of ancient petroglyph (rock carving), bone combs, ornate Indian pipes, wooden helmets and war clubs are explained in brief text.

Glubok, Shirley. **The Art of the Southwest Indians**. Macmillan, 1971.

Useful photographs provide ideas about basketweaving, sandpainting, rock pictures and Kachina masks. Tribes are defined and credit given to particular tribe.

Greenlee, Donna. **The Navajo Design Book**. Fund Publishing Company, P.O. Box 2049, Scottsdale, Arizona 85252.

Fosters appreciation of the designs in Indian art forms of weaving, jewelry making and sandpainting.

Grimm, William C. **Indian Harvests**. McGraw-Hill, 1977.

The land provides a rich feast. Appreciating the heritage of Indian agriculture is highlighted in this book about harvest.

Hall, Geraldine. **Kee's Home: A Beginning Navajo English Reader**. Northland, 1971.

Text in Navajo and in English depicts life in a Navajo village.

Heady, Eleanor B. **Sage Smoke: Tales of the Shoshoni-Bannoch Indians**. Follett, 1973.

A reverence for nature is expressed in these tales collected from Indians at the Fort Hall reservation.

Hesse, Zora G. **Southwestern Indian Recipe Book: Apache, Papago, Pima, Pueblo, and Navajo**. 1973. Filter Press, Box 5, Palmer Lake, Colorado 80133.

Traditional recipes for breads, stews, drinks and vegetables with a modern flair.

Hodges, Margaret. **The Fire Bringer: A Paiute Indian Legend**. Little, Brown, 1972.

An adventure in bringing fire from Burning Mountain involves a coyote and a young boy. Illustrations by Peter Parnall offer an experience in design, color and descriptive images.

Hofsinde, Robert (Gray Wolf). **Indian Arts**. Morrow, 1971.

Describes clay, copper and silver; roots, wood, stone and shell crafts. Food bowls of clay and weaving with grasses. Ideas for painting symbols on stone.

Hofsinde, Robert (Gray Wolf). **Indian Games & Crafts**. Morrow, 1967.

Two favorite areas of a culture—games and crafts. Simple diagrams for crafts are included.

Hofsinde, Robert (Gray Wolf). **Indian Music Makers**. Morrow, 1967.

Directions for making Indian musical instruments with the historical background of each.

Hofsinde, Robert (Gray Wolf). **Indian Picture Writing**. Morrow, 1959.

Examines the method the Indian used to symbolize thoughts with pictures. Children may copy symbols and create their own stories.

Hughes, Phyllis. **Pueblo Indian Cookbook: Recipes from the Pueblos of the American Southwest**. Museum of New Mexico Press, 1977.

Recipes for fry bread and frijoles included in this book of tested foods of the New Mexico Pueblos.

Hunt, Karii, and B.W. Carlson. "Indian Masks", **Masks and Mask Makers**. Abingdon Press, 1961, 26-33.

The belief that animals have spirits has prompted mask making. Each chapter on Indian masks with illustrations.

Hyde, Hazel. **Maria Making Pottery**, 1973. Sunstone Press, Box 2321, Sante Fe, New Mexico 87501.

The picture-story relates the complete process of creating a pot from clay.

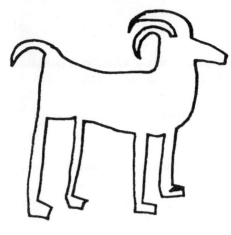

Jones, Hattie, ed. **Pottery of the North American Indians: The Trees Stand Shining**. Dial, 1971.

Significant addition to any classroom, this book of songs, prayers, lullabies and chants express a Native American view of life.

Kirk, Ruth. **David, Young Chief of the Quileutes: An American Indian Today**. Harcourt, Brace and World, 1967.

True story of Quileutes told through the life of its young chief. Tells how Indian life has been changed by the fast moving modern culture of the White man. Superb photographs of beautiful faces and places.

Krenz, Nancy and P. Byrnes. **Southwestern Arts and Crafts Projects: Ages 5-12**, 1976. Sunstone Press, Box 2321, Sante Fe, New Mexico 87501.

Activities of cultural interest for young children.

Marriott, Alice. **Winter-Telling Stories**. Crowell, 1969.

Excellent stories for dramatizing. Be selective.

Martin, Patricia Miles. **Indians: The First Americans**. Enslow Publications, 1970.

Gives general characteristics of four major tribal areas. Last chapter, "What Indians Have Given Us," is meaningful to children as they explore the culture of the "first Americans".

Mason, Bernard S. **The Book of Indian Crafts and Costumes**. Ronald Press, 1946.

A Plains Indian shield was the most valuable possession. Detailed illustration and text on how to make coup sticks, spears, calumets, quivers, pouches and dance fans. As children make these items, they gain an appreciation of the culture.

May, Julian. **Before The Indians**. Holiday House, 1969. Illustrations by Symeon Shimin.

This theoretical text is helpful when children pose questions about life before the Indians. Fantastic portrayal of Paleo-Indian by Symeon Shimin.

Parish, Peggy. **Let's Be Indians**. Harper & Row, 1962.

Resource book essential to the study of Native American culture. Describes articles from various tribes.

Payne, Elizabeth. **Meet the Native American Indians**. Random House, 1965.

Presents many facets of Indian culture. Illustrates detailed tribal activities.

Perrine, Mary. **Salt Boy**. Houghton Mifflin, 1968.

Delightful story about Indian boy's desire to learn to rope "the black horse". Illustrations capture the sensitiveness of the boy for animals.

Pine, Tillie S. **The Indians Knew**. McGraw-Hill, 1957.

Rachlis, Eugene. **Indians of the Plains**. American Heritage, 1960.

Text and illustrations describe sports and pastimes, arts, sign language, cattle, tomahawks and covered wagons.

Roessel, Robert A., Jr. and D. Platero. **Coyote Stories of the Navajo People**. Navajo Curriculum Center Press, Box 804, Blanding, Utah 84551, 1975.

Aimed at increasing understanding among all people, these stories enable Navajo children to learn about themselves and to help develop a positive self-image. The stories are related to various ceremonies and are often told in the hogan by someone from the older generation.

Showers, Paul. **Indian Festivals**. Crowell, 1969.

Describes dances of different tribes. Adapt for young children. Promotes dramatization.

Talaswaima, Terrance. **The Birds of Hano Village: A Hopi Indian Story**. Hopi Publishers, Hopi Action Program, Oraibi, Arizona 86039, 1975.

Hopi author and artist offers Indian and non-Indian a rich cultural treat. The story dramatizes the ever present need for water.

Talaswaima, Terrance. **Winter Rabbit Hunts**. Hopi Publishers, 1974.

A rabbit hunt on the Hopi reservation. Another story translated as an educational project of the Hopi Follow Through Program.

Thompson, Smith. **Tales of the North American Indians**. Indiana University Press, 1966.

Shows similarities and differences in the tales from each tribe. Read or tell the folktales. Children enjoy stories about "tricksters", "heroes" and magic.

Wolf, Bernard. **Tinker and the Medicine Men: The Story of a Navajo Boy of Monument Valley**. Random House, 1973.

The traditional religious customs are observed by the Yazzie family. Book emphasizes preservation of lifestyle of Navajo Nation and enables children to recognize the values of the Navajo.

The children at the Learning Tree also enjoy these stories. Look for them in your library.

Baldwin, Gordon C., **Games of the American Indian**
Bauer, Helen, **California Indian Days**
Bealer, Alex W., **The Picture Skin Story**
Chafetz, Henry, **Thunderbird and Other Stories**
Clark, Ann N., **The Desert People**
Clark, Ann N., **The Little Indian Basket Maker**
Clark, Ann N., **In My Mother's House**
Holling, C., **The Book of Indians**
Hunt, Ben W., **Golden Book of Indian Crafts and Lore**

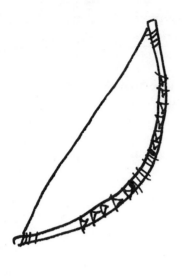

Kirk, Ruth, **David, Young Chief of the Quileutes: An American Indian Today**

Kobrin, Janet and M. Bernstein, **How the Sun Made a Promise and Kept It: A Canadian Indian Myth**

Lacotawin, Rosebud Y.R., **An Album of American Indians**

La Farge, Olivia, **The American Indian**

La Farge, Olivia, **A Pictorial History of the American Indian**

Martini, Teri, **The True Book of Indians**

McGraw, Jessie B., **Painted Pony Runs Away**

McNeer, May, **The Story of the Southwest**

Moon, Grace and C., **One Little Indian**

Sleator, William, **The Angry Moon**

Sutton, Felix, **The How and Why Wonder Book of North American Indians**

Thompson, Hildegard, **Getting to Know American Indians Today**

Tomkins, William, **Indian Sign Language**

Warren, Betsy, **Indians: Who Lived in Texas**

Williams, Barbara, **Let's Go to an Indian Cliff Dwelling**

Books for Adults

Adams, William, Ed., Momaday, **American Indian Authors**, Houghton Mifflin, 1972.

"Indians used words with reverence, weaving them into chants and songs to create beauty and to express their daily needs and aspirations." Excerpts from the oral traditions. Authors range from Black Elk to Vine Deloria.

Art and Indian Children, 1970, Curriculum Bulletin No. 7, Pima-Papago-Apache, Center for the Arts of Indian Americans, 1700 Pennsylvania Avenue, NW, Washington, DC 20006.

Resource on American Indian art. Written to help Indian children discover their potential for art expression. Many photographs help understanding about how art is done and how this art has its beginning in nature.

Bleeker, Sonia. **Indians of the Longhouse: The Story of the Iroquois**. Morrow, 1950.

Excellent resource. Gives detail about this woodland tribe.

Costo, Rupert, ed., **Textbooks and the American Indian**, American Indian Historical Society, 1969. Indian Historian Press, 1451 Masonic Avenue, San Francisco, CA 94117

Source for evaluating books about American Indians. Criteria for judging these books are excellent.

Dance with Indian Children, 1972, Center for the Arts of Indian Americans, 1700 Pennsylvania Avenue, NW, Washington, DC 20006.

Developed through the American Indian Culture Heritage Education and the Arts for teachers of Indian children. Photographs, description and poetry are clear so that all children can learn the dances and the meaning of the movements.

Dunn, Lynn P., **American Indians: A Study Guide and Sourcebook**, R & E, 1975.

Brief history about the identity, conflict and integration/nationalism of the Native Americans from 1700 to the 1970's. Additional references listed.

Erdoes, Richard. **The Sun Dance People**. Knopf, 1972.

Past and present of Plains Indians. Vivid photographs.

Gridley, Marion E., **Indian Tribes of America**. Rand-McNally, 1973.

The American Indian must be presented to children by tribe since each tribe has a special culture. For young children, use the Indian tribe which lived, or still lives, in your area.

Gridley, Marion E., **Contemporary Indian Leaders**. Dodd, 1972.

Use this book to acquaint children with Indians who are living in your region today.

Keegan, Marcia. **Pueblo and Navajo Cookery**. Earth Books. 1977.

These recipes, photographs, and statements are representative of the nineteen Indian Pueblos in New Mexico and the vast Navajo Nation in northern Arizona.

A Kindergarten Curriculum Guide for Indian Children: A Bilingual-Bicultural Approach, U.S. Department of the Interior, Bureau of Indian Affairs, Indian Education Resources Center, 123 Fourth Street SW, Albuquerque, NM 87103.

Songs and many other activities, with photographs of Indian children today.

Klein, Barry T., **Reference Encyclopedia of the American Indian**, Volume 1, 2nd ed., Todd, 1973.

Most complete collection of sources about the American Indian. Materials on all aspects of Indian life — museums, monuments, urban centers, craft shops — and many more.

Laxalt, Robert. "New Mexico: the Golden Lands", **National Geographic**, 138, (September, 1970), 299-343.

New Mexico remains the home of 77,000 Indians. What it is like to live in New Mexico, striving to retain their cultural heritage, is explored in this article.

Looney, Ralph. "The Navajos", **National Geographic**, 142, (December, 1972), 741-481.

The invasion by White man, a history of broken treaties, neglect and exploration finds modern Navajos still coping with prejudice and unemployment. The traditional reverence for land yields to economic pressures.

Louis Ray B., **Child of the Hogan**, Brigham Young University Press, 1975.

The hope of the Navajo child of today is beautifully expressed through poetry and short stories, accompanied by photographs of Navajo life today.

McLuhan, Terry C. (comp) **Touch the Earth**. S & S, 1976.

Passages written by Indians. Emphasis on the importance of harmony between man and nature.

Morey, Sylvester M. and O.L. Gilliam, eds., **Respect for Life**, Waldorf Press, 1974.

"For a long time Indian parents have protested against rearing their young as though they were white children." Authors examine traditional Indian views of child rearing and education, a subject not considered since 1744. Based on interviews with Native Americans.

Navajo Community College Press, Many Farms Rural Route, Chinle, Arizona 86503.

Navajo Curriculum Center, Rough Rock Demonstration School, Chinle, Arizona 86503.

Navajo Tribal Museum, P.O. Box 797, Window Rock, Arizona 86515.

Bibliographies, articles, information. Sources for materials.

Niethammer, Carolyn, **American Indian Food and Lore**, Macmillan, 1974.

150 recipes from Indian women from a number of Indian tribes. Also a study of plants used in these recipes. Information about plants and botany is accurate as well as how to prepare the plants for cooking.

Thompson, Hildegard, **The Navajos Long Walk For Education**, Navajo College Press, 1975.

Only recently have the Navajos developed education that includes their own culture.

Thomas, Marjorie, comp., **Indian Cultural Units for the Classroom**, Indian Cultural Curriculum Center, 1975. Tuba City Public Schools, Tuba City, AZ 86045.

Units are arranged by Indian tribes. Includes music, games, clothing and other aspects of Indian life. Rich resource for Indian cultures.

Whitney, Alex, **Sports and Games the Indians Gave Us**, McKay, 1977.

Many types of games are explained. Games with balls, guessing games, water sports, acrobatic contests—and many more. Simple instructions with illustrations for making the equipment.

Magazines

Man and His Music
(Special issue on the American Indian, January, 1972.)
Quarterly
Keyboard Jr. Publications, 1346 Chapel Street, New Haven, CO 16511

Eight-page magazine for appreciation of music for children ages 5 through 12. Issues feature composers, musicians, music, and types of music. Excellent background information to use with children.

Indian Trader
Bi-monthly
H. Guy, P.O. Box 867, Gallup, NM 85701.

History and culture of Amerindian art, customs and Indian tribes. Arts and crafts, exhibitions, shows and programs are advertised.

Wee Wish Tree
7 issues a year
American Indian Historical Society, 1451 Masonic Avenue, San Francisco, CA 94117

Magazine of Native American cultures for young people. Poems by natives about Indian cultures and games, pictures of Indians in authentic dress and articles on art.

Records and Films

Canyon Records, 4143 North Sixteenth Street, Phoenix, Arizona 85016.

Records, cassettes, transparencies, study guides, photographs, maps and bibliography about the Native American. One of few sources for authentic American Indian music. Write for catalog.

"Indian Songs of the Southwest". Thunderbird Records. Sante Fe, New Mexico 87501. Record TBR1943B

The music of the Southwest Native Americans is related to their religion and tribal life.

Native American Arts. Dist: Modern Talking Picture Service, 2323 New Park Road, Hyde Park, New York 11040

A panoramic survey of the development of Native American artists and their works from prehistoric to contemporary times.

"Shee-nasha", **Little Johnny Brown**, with Ella Jenkins. Dist: Scholastic Records, 906 Sylvan Avenue, Englewood Cliffs, New Jersey 07632.

A Navajo song taught to Ella Jenkins by children on the Navajo Reservation in Arizona. Children learn this song quickly.

Sounds of Indian America: Plains and Southwest. Dist: Indian House, Box 472, Taos, New Mexico 87571. Record 87557 Record 87557

Variety of music from several tribes has been recorded. Booklet included describes dances with large photographs.

SELECTED BIBLIOGRAPHY
Multi-Cultural Resources

Books for Children

Adoff, Arnold. **Black Is Brown Is Tan**. Harper & Row, 1973.

Integration in a family is dealt with in a positive manner. Fills the void of books that deal with racial differences in marriage.

Baylor, Byrd. **The Way to Start a Day**. Scribner's, 1978.

"A morning needs to be sung to. A new day needs to be honored." Beautiful illustrations complement this book about how people all over the world have paid their respects to the wonder of each new surprise.

Bond, Jean Carey. **Brown Is A Beautiful Color**. Watts, 1969.

Two Black artists present the pleasurable experience of the color brown.

Buffet, Guy and P. **Adventures of Kama Pua**. Island Heritage, 1972.

Watercolor paintings with a text of Hawaiian names retell a story about magic.

Buffet, Guy and P. **Pua Pua Lena Lena and the Magic Ki ha-Pu**. Island Heritage, 1972.

An adventure about a thirty-foot dog and how he brings peace to the valley.

Cooper, Terry and M. Ratner. **Many Hands Cooking: An International Cookbook for Boys and Girls**. UNICEF, Crowell, 1974.

Recipes from all over the world.

Hautzig, Ester. **At Home: A Visit in Four Languages**. Illustrated by Aliki. MacMillan, 1969. **In School: Learning in Four Languages**. Illustrated by Nonny Hogrogian. MacMillan, 1969. **In the Park: An Excursion in Four Languages**. Illustrated by Ezra Jack Keats. MacMillan, 1969.

Set of books in four languages—Spanish, English, Russian and French.

Heide, Florence Parry. **My Castle**. McGraw-Hill, 1972.

A young child reacts to being left alone all day. Symeon Shimin creates a beautiful "castle" with his watercolor and pencil sketches.

Simon, Norma. **Why Am I Different?** Albert Whitman, 1979.

Explores some of the aspects of human existence that makes each person special. Comparisons are drawn regarding height, weight, hair color, taste in food, family racial and cultural backgrounds.

Zim, Jacob, ed. **My Shalom My Peace: Paintings and Poems by Jewish and Arab Children**. McGraw-Hill, 1974.

Children's poems illustrated with numerous line drawings and half tones.

Books and Resources for Adults

About Us: The Childcraft Annual, Field Enterprises Educational Corporation, 1973.

Explores cultures of "the people of the planet earth." Categorizes them by colors, sizes, shapes and different ways of life. Photographs are authentic and artistic.

Anti-Defamation League of B'nai B'rith, Book Department, 315 Lexington Avenue, New York, NY 10016.

Publishes books, pamphlets and films on many cultures. Materials for children and adults. Purpose of the league is to promote peace and harmony among all cultures, especially in the United States. Write for list of publications. Check telephone directory for regional office.

Bowmar, 622 Rodier Drive, Glendale, CA 91201.

Request catalog of multicultural materials. Publishes posters, music, books and other materials.

Cashman, Marc, ed., **Bibliography of American Ethnology**, Bicentennial 1st ed., Todd, 1976.

A rich source for books and other materials for American Indians, Black Americans and other minorities.

Children and Intercultural Education, 1973, Association for Childhood Education International, 3615 Wisconsin Avenue, NW, Washington, DC 20016.

Three booklets for teachers with many ideas to promote cultural pluralism and acceptance of diversity.

The Children of This World, UNICEF, the 4th World Exhibition of Photography, Stern, 1977.

Purpose of exhibit was to improve human awareness of all cultures. Photographs of children from 52 countries. They show joys and sorrows, and plenty and poverty. "The welfare of today's children is inseparably linked with the peace of tomorrow."

A Child's Cook Book, 656 Terra California Drive #3, Walnut Creek, CA 94595.

Recipes for foods popular with young children. Recipes from many cultures. Each recipe is for an individual serving and has both words and pictures. Pre-readers can follow recipes by themselves.

Cohen, Robert, **The Color of Man**, Random House, 1968.

Ken Heyman photographed people in black and white from many cultures. Text was researched by experts in each field. Shows beauty of life in each culture.

Cole, Ann and others, **Children Are Children Are Children**, Little, Brown, 1978.

An activity approach to exploring Brazil, France, Iran, Japan, Nigeria and the USSR.

Colorado Gold, Colorado Association for the Education of Young Children, 1788 Geneva Street, Aurora, CO 80010.

Recipes of Indian, Mexican, Asian and Soul food. Also rhymes, songs and creative art activities.

Council on Interracial Books for Children, Inc., 1841 Broadway, New York, NY 10023.

Publishes a Bulletin and other publications and filmstrips. Is an effort to eliminate racism in American society. Good reviews of new books and materials on cultures.

Early Childhood Bookhouse, 108 NW 9th, Suite 206, Portland, OR 97209.

Early childhood books from many publishers. Good selection. Request catalog.

ERIC Clearinghouse for Elementary and Early Childhood Education, University of Illinois, College of Education, Urbana, IL 61801.

Many bibliographies on current publications are available for low cost. Will do ERIC search on a topic for a fee. See **Resources in Education** for publications on all topics listed with ERIC.

Ethnic Chronology Series: Chronology and Fact Books, Oceana, 1971.

A sixteen-volume history of ethnic groups.

Farrell, Edmund J. and others, **I/You — We/They**, Scott, Foresman, 1976.

Literature by and about ethnic groups. Helps grasp the essence of a multicultural nation. Many ethnic authors and poets represented.

Guidelines for Selecting Bias-Free Textbooks and Storybooks, Council on Interracial Books for Children, 1980. Address above.

Guidelines to evaluate many kinds of materials used in educating children. Goal of Council is to assist in selecting books that are authentic. Excellent source.

Gryphon House, Early Childhood Books, P.O. Box 217, Mt. Rainier, MD 20822.

Early childhood books from many publishers. Good selection. Request catalog.

Information Center on Children's Cultures, U.S. Committee for UNICEF, 331 East 38th Street, New York, NY 10016.

Educational and cultural materials for children up to age nine from different countries. Request catalog. Check telephone directory for local representative.

Institute of Texan Cultures, P.O. Box 1226, San Antonio, TX 78206.

Continues to publish booklets, posters and slides/filmstrips about the many cultures which settled in Texas. Combines photographs with brief text. Some available in Spanish. Traveling exhibits available. Excellent and authentic materials. Request list of publications. Visit the exhibitions and see the films at the institute. Attend the annual folk festival in August.

Krenz, Nancy and P. Byrnes, **Southwestern Arts and Crafts Projects**, Ages 5-12. Sunstone Press, 1976.

Illustrated activities for the Mexican and Indian cultures.

Locketz, Louise, **Careers in Actions/Minorities in Focus**, St. Paul Public Schools, Career Education, MN, 1977. Pub. 76770194.

Photographs with text on career close-ups of Asian Americans, Black, Chicanos and Native Americans in the twin cities.

Mason, Jerry, ed., **The Family of Children**, Ridge Press, Grosset and Dunlap, 1977.

Black and white photographs of children around the world from 71 countries. Pictures of children growing up, playing; also schools, games and other activities; and all the human feelings.

Miller, Carl S., **Sing Children Sing: Songs, Dances and Singing Games of Many Lands and Peoples**, Time Books, 1972. Distributed by Quadrangle/New York Times.

Music, illustrated with photographs, representing many different cultures.

Multicultural Aspects of American Life and Education: An Annotated Bibliography, Multilingual Assessment Program, New York Component, 1976. Available from Center for Bilingual Bicultural Education, 7703 North Lamar, Austin, TX 78752.

Extensive information on bilingual and cultural aspects of Mexican Americans, Puerto Ricans, Cubans, Black Americans, Native Americans and other ethnic groups.

National Geographic Magazine, published by the National Geographic Society, 17th and M Streets NW, Washington, DC 20036.

The magazine is an excellent source for articles and beautiful colored photographs from countries all over the world. The Society also publishes a magazine for children, titled "World."

Perspectives on School Print Materials: Ethnic, Non-sexist and Others, STRIDE, Far West Laboratory of Educational Research and Development, 1855 Folsom Road, San Francisco, CA 94103.

Information for evaluating school materials about the Native American, Black Americans and Chinese Americans.

Rainbow Activities, The Ethnic Cultural Heritage Program, 1977, Creative Teaching Press, South El Monte, CA 91733.

Activities developed to encourage appreciation of cultural heritage of all children. Fifty multicultural human relations experiences. A few are suitable for young children. Use them with groups of adults.

Schmidt, Velma E. and E. McNeill, **Cultural Awareness**, 1978, National Association for the Education of Young Children, 1834 Connecticut Avenue NW, Washington, DC 20009.

An annotated bibliography of books for children and adults; of materials including posters, audiovisuals, dolls, arts and crafts, museums and ceremonial events. These cultures are included: Asian American, Black American, Native American, and Spanish Speaking Americans. Also multicultural materials.

Shephard, Mary and R., **Vegetable Soup Activities**, illustrated with characters from the TV show, Citation Press, 1975.

Many related activities. Detailed instructions for making pinatas, origami birds, other crafts, ethnic recipes, games around the world, and much more.

Spicer, Dorothy G., **The Book of Festivals**, Gale Research Company, 1969.

Cultural background of folk customs of many peoples represented through their festivals, are described.

Thernstrom, Stephan ed., **Harvard Encyclopedia of American Ethnic Groups**. Harvard University Press. 1980.

Provides the first comprehensive and systematic review of the many peoples of this country.

U.S. Toy Company, 2008 W. 103rd Terrace, Leawood, Kansas 66206.
Excellent books, games and supplies. Numerous cultural resources.

Wasserman, Paul J. and J. Morgan, eds., **Ethnic Information Sources of the United States**, Gale Research Company, 1976.

Comprehensive reference for many ethnic organizations and businesses. Black Americans, Native Americans and Eskimos are **not** included.

Wasserman, Paul J. and others, eds., **Festivals Sourcebook**, Gale Research Company, 1977.

Lists information for more than 3800 festivals, fairs and community celebrations in the United States and Canada. Field trip guide for your community.

Werner, Emily E., **Cross-Cultural Child Development**, Brooks/ Cole, 1979.

Synthesis of knowledge about the physical, cognitive and social development of children who live in the developing countries. Book for the researcher.

Wynar, Lubomyr R., **Encyclopedic Directory of Ethnic Organizations in the United States**, Libraries Unlimited, 1975.

Source for organizations committed to improving life for minorities.